BUILDING SPIRITUAL MUSCLE

A SIX-WEEK JOURNEY TO SHAPE A MORE POWERFUL FAITH

SABRINA N. SHORT & CHRIS WILTERDINK

ISBNs
978-0-88177-862-5 (print)
978-0-88177-863-2 (mobi)
978-0-88177-864-9 (ePub)

DR862

TABLE OF CONTENTS

WELCOME

The Division on Ministries with Young People (DMYP) at Discipleship Ministries exists to support and challenge the local church in disciple making. One way to define *discipleship* is "a journey toward spiritual maturity." Physical maturity in youth is easy to see. Spiritual maturity may not be as obvious. Vital churches understand that developing and recognizing spiritual maturity in young people is a key component of their own vitality. This resource provides a training plan for youth to practice their faith, build spiritual maturity, and develop their potential to become Christian leaders.

God's unearned grace blesses our lives. John Wesley called the followers of the Methodist movement to live active lives as a response to that freely given grace. Just like an athlete who trains his or her body for a game, or an intellectual who trains his or her mind for a test, faith can be exercised, strengthened, and developed. Olympic athletes build muscle, enlist coaches, create strategies, and practice for years before those quadrennial games. Marathon runners don't just wake up one day and decide to run more than twenty-six miles; they begin with running small distances then gradually build up their endurance and strength. Likewise, the Christian life is a marathon, not a sprint. The authors of the book of Hebrews and Philippians knew this (Hebrews 12:1-15 and Philippians 3:12-16). Those Christians seeking spiritual maturity can practice their faith to build strength and endurance. Endurance comes through developing habits and methods that strengthen their life of discipleship. Spiritual training, just like physical exercise, is most successful with a commitment to regular practice, support from a community, encouragement from dependable sources, and a goal in mind.

Using this resource as a part of youth ministry will provide opportunities for discipleship, encouragement from United Methodist leaders, and create a community of support. The video pieces (available online at https://umcyoungpeople.org/spiritualmuscle) were part of presentations at YOUTH 2015, the national event for United Methodist youth in the United States. The YOUTH event takes place every four years. YOUTH 2015 challenged participants to "Go On" and grow toward spiritual maturity in their walk with Christ (Hebrews 6:1). Young Christians, youth leaders, and clergy heard from phenomenal United Methodist speakers at that event.

During the event, youth were inspired to practice spiritual disciplines by incorporating Wesleyan principles in their daily lives. Learning about the principles is only the first step. What does a Christian need to do to be strong in the journey? How do we build our spiritual muscles for the work? What must we do to have genuine and authentic relationship with God?

Building Spiritual Muscle will motivate and encourage youth to continue their journey of being followers of Christ by building their stamina for the road ahead. In this six-week study, each one-hour lesson will focus on key characteristics for staying the course, strengthening our faith, and reconnecting to purpose through weekly spiritual workouts. The study will explore the Wesleyan works of piety and mercy through video segments, written reflections, and exercises designed for participants to begin living out their faith in a real and tangible way.

Speakers featured in the clips are "trainers" to help shape a more powerful faith. They push us to step out on our faith and push the limits of our Christian experience.

Many people contributed to the effort to make this resource a reality. I would like to thank Sabrina Short, Chris Wilterdink, Anthony Burns, Wendy Mohler-Seib as writers, video editors, and collaborators on this resource as well as offer a special thank you to the design teams throughout the years for the national YOUTH event. Thank you to all who make a difference in the lives of youth!

> So then let's also run the race that is laid out in front of us, since we have such a great cloud of witnesses surrounding us. Let's throw off any extra baggage, get rid of the sin that trips us up, and fix our eyes on Jesus, faith's pioneer and perfecter. He endured the cross, ignoring the shame, for the sake of the joy that was laid out in front of him, and sat down at the right side of God's throne.
>
> Think about the one who endured such opposition from sinners so that you won't be discouraged and you won't give up. In your struggle against sin, you haven't resisted yet to the point of shedding blood, and you have forgotten the encouragement that addresses you as sons and daughters:
>
> *My child, don't make light of the Lord's discipline*
> *or give up when you are corrected by him,*
> *because the Lord disciplines whomever he loves,*
> *and he punishes every son or daughter whom he accepts.*
>
> Bear hardship for the sake of discipline. God is treating you like sons and daughters! What child isn't disciplined by his or her father? But if you don't experience discipline, which happens to all children, then you are illegitimate and not real sons and daughters. What's more, we had human parents who disciplined us, and we respected them for it. How much more should we submit to the Father of spirits and live? Our human parents disciplined us for a little while,

as it seemed best to them, but God does it for our benefit so that we can share his holiness. No discipline is fun while it lasts, but it seems painful at the time. Later, however, it yields the peaceful fruit of righteousness for those who have been trained by it.

So strengthen your drooping hands and weak knees! Make straight paths for your feet so that if any part is lame, it will be healed rather than injured more seriously. Pursue the goal of peace along with everyone—and holiness as well, because no one will see the Lord without it. Make sure that no one misses out on God's grace. Make sure that no root of bitterness grows up that might cause trouble and pollute many people. (Hebrews 12:1-15, CEB)

"It's not that I have already reached this goal or have already been perfected, but I pursue it, so that I may grab hold of it because Christ grabbed hold of me for just this purpose. Brothers and sisters, I myself don't think I've reached it, but I do this one thing: I forget about the things behind me and reach out for the things ahead of me. The goal I pursue is the prize of God's upward call in Christ Jesus. So all of us who are spiritually mature should think this way, and if anyone thinks differently, God will reveal it to him or her. Only let's live in a way that is consistent with whatever level we have reached" (Philippians 3:12-16).

VIDEO TRAINER BIOS

Rev. Cedrick Bridgeforth, EdD, serves as an ordained elder in the California-Pacific Conference of The United Methodist Church. He is a native of Alabama, a US Air Force veteran, and graduate of Samford University (Birmingham, AL), Claremont School of Theology (Claremont, CA), and Pepperdine University (Malibu, CA).

Rev. Bridgeforth's service to the church began at an early age, and his appointment history includes pastorates in Los Angeles (Bowen Memorial UMC and Crenshaw UMC), Santa Ana, CA (Santa Ana UMC), and an appointment as a district superintendent. He served as director of alumni and church relations at Claremont School of Theology and chaired Black Methodists for Church Renewal. He is a faithful member of Alpha Phi Alpha Fraternity, Inc.

Rev. Olu Brown is the founder and lead pastor of Impact Church in Atlanta, Georgia. He is married to Farrah Brown, and they are the proud parents of Daya Brown. A native of Texas, Olu graduated from The Interdenominational Theological Center in Atlanta, and he was associate pastor at Cascade United Methodist Church for six years prior to starting Impact Church.

Impact Church is committed to sharing the love of Christ with the world and reaching all people who want to realize their God-given potential. They serve a diverse congregation of all ages, backgrounds, and interests.

Rev. Telley Gadson calls South Carolina home. She graduated from Candler School of Theology at Emory University in Atlanta. Pastor T serves on the NAACP Board of Directors Religious Affairs Committee, has been a delegate to General Conference, and has preached for local congregations, annual conference gatherings, and been a special guest at the White House. Yet perhaps most important, Pastor T patterns her life after this saying: "If I can help somebody as I travel along the way, then my living shall not be in vain."

Taylor Ogden Thomas is the middle-school minister at the United Methodist Church of the Resurrection in Leawood, Kansas. While spending a year overseas doing mission work before college, Taylor heard the call to pursue ministry and trusted that God would use her wherever she landed. Now fifteen years has passed, and God continues to challenge her to respond and live into that call. She has served three churches in her career in youth ministry and has been serving at Church of the Resurrection for the last eleven years with an intentional focus on middle-school ministries.

Taylor is passionate about students, families, and relational ministry. Her love of people is rooted in growing up in a family that was focused on choosing joy and laughter. Taylor carries on this joy in her marriage to Lance Thomas and raising their three little boys, Camp, Crew, and Cutler (and don't forget their dog, Major).

Rev. Mike Slaughter, lead pastor at Ginghamsburg Church, is in his fourth decade as the chief dreamer of this congregation. His lifelong passion to reach the lost and set the oppressed free has now made him a tireless and leading advocate for the children, women, and men of Darfur, Sudan. Under Mike's leadership, Ginghamsburg Church has become known as an early innovator of small-group ministry, the church "media reformation," and cyberministry. In 2007, *The Church Report* listed Mike as one of the "top 50 most influential Christians in America."

Mike travels globally to speaking engagements and uses his "gift of irritation" to equip ministry leaders to minimize brick and maximize mission so that they may fully deploy the mission of Jesus into the world. He is also the author of multiple books including *Dare to Dream*; *Shiny Gods*; *Christmas Is Not Your Birthday: Experience the Joy of Living and Giving Like Jesus*; and *Change the World: Recovering the Message and Mission of Jesus*, all published by Abingdon Press.

Rev. Sam Yun (also known as "P. Sam") is an ordained elder in the California-Pacific Annual Conference of The United Methodist Church. P. Sam has served as minister of young adults at Los Altos Hills UMC in Northern California and works with Embrace Church. Father of two, lover of all sports with a net (even badminton), follower of Jesus, he is a man immensely broken but constantly healed and strengthened by the love and grace of God. P. Sam's most important theological faith conviction is simply this: "If God can love the likes of me, God can love anyone." P. Sam is always open to talk about this with anyone who's interested.

OVERVIEW: BUILDING SPIRITUAL MUSCLE

This resource contains two different sets of scripts: A "Trainer's Script" and a "Coach's Playbook."

The Trainer's Script is a fully scheduled and scripted set of instructions, including suggestions for activities and what to say, laid out in six hour-long sessions.

The Coach's Playbook shares only the core "Session Elements" for each of the six sessions. The playbook invites creativity and allows for increased flexibility in session content, organized by the group leader.

Trainer's Script

A trainer's knowledge of the group and spiritual exercises work hand in hand. A trainer guides participants through workout sessions and spiritual exercises. A trainer participates fully in the exercises with others in the group, while at the same time leading the group through the session.

The Trainer Script is ideal for:

- groups of twelve or fewer participants
- adult leaders who want significant detail and direction
- adult leaders who want to exercise themselves and participate in the experience
- leaders who want to help equip participants with new skills
- youth wanting to lead one another through the experience
- groups who need help defining their spiritual growth goals
- groups who consider themselves at or near the beginning of their spiritual journey

Coach's Playbook

A coach has knowledge and provides direction. He or she has a playbook and asks that participants be willing to put in the work and take ownership of their own development. This script is ideal for:

- larger groups that can break down into smaller discussion groups
- adult leaders who want a few plays in their playbook, but want the freedom to put together their own sessions from the suggested exercises
- leaders who want participants to take ownership for their own goals and spiritual development
- groups that already have some spiritual strength or maturity
- groups that want to take their spiritual exercise to a higher level

Session Elements

Each spiritual workout session focuses on different practices that will strengthen different aspects of a person's spiritual muscle. By completing each session, youth will build new spiritual muscles and learn new spiritual disciplines. Balance and moderation are good things; doing only one exercise all the time can cause fatigue and exhaustion. Varied spiritual workouts will stretch and strengthen different elements of faith. Each workout session is composed of six elements. These six elements focus conversation and activities on different topics, depending on the theme of the week.

Each session in both the Trainer's Script and Coach's Playbook contains the following elements:

- **Foundations:** Engaging scripture. Reading and studying the Bible was central to John Wesley's understanding of the Christian journey. Wrestling with scripture is encouraged. The core muscles in our physical bodies are the muscles that keep us balanced and enable us to do everything that we do. Engaging scripture builds our core spiritual muscles, which helps us stay balanced and align our beliefs and actions. Scripture can (and should) be an everyday source of inspiration and contemplation. Each lesson contains a scripture connected to the weekly theme and focus. Read the Foundations passage at the beginning of each session to provide supporting scripture to guide activities and discussions. Encourage youth participants to repeat the reading of each scripture between lessons and reflect upon the different reactions they have to the scripture throughout the week.
- **Reflection:** *The FaithMinder Journal* is a companion resource designed for your group's participants to use along with your weekly sessions for *Building Spiritual Muscle. The FaithMinder Journal* (ISBN: 978-0-88177-865-6) is a downloadable PDF available for purchase through The Upper Room Bookstore (Bookstore.UpperRoom.org; 1-800-972-0433). Participants will use the journal between sessions to answer questions, record their activity and thoughts, and pay attention to

where they invest their time. The journal will help build awareness about spiritual fitness. Journal time is incorporated into the sessions for introspection. The group leader will guide the journaling through focused questions. These questions help individuals meditate on how the key principles for the week relate to their own lives. Participants are encouraged to give themselves at least fifteen minutes each week to examine God's Word through personal journaling. They may write lyrics or poems, or they may draw—encourage them to be creative! Private entries do not have to be shared with the group, but students may decide to share as a part of group discussion.

- **Inspire:** Each "Inspire" video clip (available online at https://umcyoungpeople.org/spiritual muscle) features main stage speakers from the YOUTH event in 2015. These conversations inspire youth to go on toward Christian maturity while teaching inward and outward expressions of our faith. The clips provide context in each session and provide direction for the theme. Leaders have access to the full version of each presenter's full talks with the purchase of the resource. Leaders are welcome to use additional video, beyond the identified and edited clips, if they so choose.
- **Share:** Discussion questions are woven into different session elements. These are designed to facilitate conversation and to help people engage with one another. Structured for small-group settings, these sessions enable youth leaders and youth to build a supportive community that encourages spiritual growth. If used in a large-group setting, these questions are best addressed by breaking into smaller groups. The questions could also be modified for use during the week by participants in their *FaithMinder Journal.* "Share" questions are divided into three groups based on their intensity level. Use, combine, and create questions that will be best for your group. Assess which questions are best for your ministry setting and group ahead of time. The three groups of questions are:
    - **Exploring Faith**: These **Exploring** questions may be most appropriate for those youth who are new to Christianity, haven't made a commitment to Christ, or who feel like they are starting from scratch. They are low-risk, easy-lifting questions that invite responses. They include questions about new knowledge of the Bible, growth in a faith community, and reflect a basic understanding of Christ's message. Consider these as introductory or beginner level questions.
    - **Following the Path**: These **Following** questions may be appropriate for those who have already made a commitment to live as a disciple, following the example of Jesus Christ, and have some familiarity with spiritual disciplines and the church. These heavier questions encourage further faith formation, building confidence in God, and stretching spiritual muscles into the world as a follower of Jesus. These questions will help youth discover their gifts and service for worship. Consider these the intermediate or medium-level questions.
    - **Leading the Way**: These **Leading** questions may be appropriate for those already strong in their faith and in the Word, ready to take their faith and become leaders in their church and

community. These heavyweight questions will challenge participants to think about their actions and how they can help lift others to a life in Christ. These questions work spiritual muscles for evangelism. Becoming a world-changing disciple means sharing the Word and transforming the world as you are transformed. This is the most advanced level of questions.

- **Motivate:** These video clips (available at https://umcyoungpeople.org/spiritualmuscle) showcase the diverse group of main speakers from worship at the YOUTH event in 2015. "Motivate" videos help complete the exercise circuit for each session. Each clip encourages all participants to move forward, stay focused, and be the light. Clips can be used at any point during the session, and they function well as a transition between discussions or writing exercises. The video clips reinforce the topic for the session and spur ongoing reflection and activity during the upcoming week. Full versions of each talk are available to leaders when they have purchased the resource. Just like the "Inspire" video clips, leaders are welcome to view and use more of each talk as they determine what is best for their ministry context and participants.
- **Spiritual Workout:** These are the activities for individuals to complete during the week, between group sessions. This is where the most spiritual muscle gets built—from regular, committed activity that then can be shared in a supportive community. After groups have met, individuals can put what they learn to action on their own. Each weekly workout invites the group to implement and practice spiritual disciplines as a part of daily life. These individual workouts are also grouped into the same three levels as the "Share" questions: exploring, following, and leading.
  - **Exploring** level activities are the lightest level, with activities only a few days per week.
  - **Following** level activities represent an "almost every day" set of commitments.
  - **Leading** level activities require an everyday commitment.

PREMEETING SCALES

In exercise, knowledge is power. A key part of building spiritual muscle, just like improving physical fitness or learning any new skill, is tracking growth and development over time. Before jumping into the *Building Spiritual Muscle* workout sessions, each participant should complete some of the premeeting scales. This will help participants recognize their beginning activity levels and understandings of faith, track their growth through the six sessions, and allow them to reflect on their growth at the end of the six weeks. Trainers and coaches are welcome to combine the suggested scales here, or even create their own scales!

The group leader can help determine which scales and measurements are best for the group. The leader should consider the spiritual maturity of youth participants before choosing which scales to recommend. Leaders can also use the premeeting scales after the sessions are finished as a way to measure growth and how the participants in the group met their goals or how they changed over the course of the study.

Participants can use the scales as an introduction to Week One as their baseline activity level and their current state of belief. These can be helpful reference points as they exercise their faith and make new connections between their spirituality and their actions.

Measurement Scales (Available in Appendix)

- Faith Maturity Scale
- Religious Behavior Scale
- Personal Holiness Activity Tracker
- Social Holiness Activity Tracker
- Church Familiarity Scale
- Community Familiarity Scale

Week 1: Believe God

TRAINER'S SCRIPT

Supplies

Bible
FaithMinder Journal
Internet access and computer
Variety of nutritional snacks (optional)
Writing paper, writing utensils, and envelopes

The youth will come into this session having reflected on their baseline activity level and personal goals for their time in this study. Spend a little time reviewing any completed premeeting scales and personal goals, as this is the first in-person meeting for the group. Introduce and catch up with one another (remind one another of names/schools/etc. if your group doesn't know one another well yet). Christianity, after all, is a social religion! Provide space for youth to share their goals with one another.

As a trainer, you have valuable knowledge and will be a hands-on guide for the youth in your group. You will practice the same exercises that they do, walking with them over the next several weeks as they discover the differences that active faith can create in the Christian life. Knowledge is power in exercise. During this study, know your own goals and limits in addition to those of your youth. Create knowledge by tracking your activity and faithfully doing those things you've committed to do. Finally, make sure to have rest and reflection periods where you can look over what you have tracked to see your own growth and the growth in your youth.

Guide the discussion to help participants think about what they already know about God, Jesus, and the Holy Spirit from their own spiritual journey. Help them see where they are spiritually and identify their areas for growth. Read Matthew, chapter 5, to prepare.

As the study progresses, you will have a better idea of which level of questions is best for your group: "Exploring" (Beginner) "Following" (Intermediate) or "Leading" (Advanced).

Week 1: Believe God

TRAINER'S SCRIPT

Welcome (15 minutes)

Welcome the group. Make sure the nutritious snacks for the youth are available on a table or in a basket. Introduce yourself and set the tone and order for other introductions. Be brief and friendly; share the following information:

- Name
- Where I work/go to school
- What is your favorite snack from the available choices?
- Why am I here? What are my goals?

Invite group members to introduce themselves. These introductions should be brief and should follow a simple format, with each person sharing the same basic type of information.

After each person has introduced himself or herself, say something like:

"Thank you. The snacks are available for you to eat while we are together. Nutrition gives your body fuel to live, breathe, and exercise. Getting good food is an important part of being healthy. When we build spiritual muscle, scripture is one of our main sources of food. Digesting scripture can give us fuel for the race we run.

"Running the Christian race starts with a commitment to getting to know God better. God wants to be known. God has provided many ways for people to get to know God: engaging scripture, praying, worshiping, singing, meditating, taking Communion, and serving others, just to name a few. The ways we can get to know God are also the primary ways that God acts in our lives. God is always inviting and eager to work in us through spiritual disciplines and exercises.

"John Wesley saw scripture as primary to knowing God. Getting familiar with the Bible and learning about the life and teachings of Jesus is the foundational exercise upon which we will build everything else. Scripture is one way that we can personally get to know God. Familiarity with the life and teachings of Jesus will give us an idea of the direction we should follow as we become world-transforming disciples. Knowing God better will help us position ourselves to be transformed by God. Without direction, we can still perform good actions . . . but those actions will put us on the fast-track to nowhere. We must discover in faith where God is pointing us and trust in God's grace and will for our lives.

"We'll work together to grow toward maturity in faith. By lifting new spiritual weights, we will each grow in faith. That lifting is our response to God's free gifts of love and grace. God is the primary actor. After all, God creates the muscles, builds muscles, strengthens muscles. God transforms our spiritual muscles, especially when we position ourselves for transformation!"

Foundation (15 minutes)

Read (or have a youth read) this session's scripture:

> Don't you know that all the runners in the stadium run, but only one gets the prize? So run to win. Everyone who competes practices self-discipline in everything. The runners do this to get a crown of leaves that shrivel up and die, but we do it to receive a crown that never dies. So now this is how I run—not without a clear goal in sight. I fight like a boxer in the ring, not like someone who is shadowboxing. Rather, I'm landing punches on my own body and subduing it like a slave. I do this to be sure that I myself won't be disqualified after preaching to others. (1 Corinthians 9:24-27)

Ask two to three of the following questions:

Exploring

- What kinds of races, or competitions, do you know where only the first-place person gets a prize?
- Why do people compete in those kinds of races (especially if they are not paid professionals)?
- What do you think "the crown that never dies" means?
- What is self-discipline?
- What kind of training/practice would help someone win a running race?

Following

- What is the difference between running with a clear goal and running without a clear goal?
- Why is self-discipline important to a Christian?
- What do you think self-discipline and being a disciple have in common?
- Why do you think the author (Paul) talks about fighting with himself and subduing his body?
- What things help you run the race of your life as a Christian?

Leading

- Do you believe that those who run "God's race" do so to get a prize?
- What is the goal of living life as a Christian?
- What goals do you see your friends running toward?
- What goals keep Christians motivated? What goals keep *you* motivated to continue growing in faith?
- How does the difficult, behind the scenes kind of training prepare you for the choices you make in public?

Inspire (15 minutes) "Here to There"

Using your computer/TV/screen and internet connection, watch Inspire Clip 1 at https://umcyoungpeople.org/spiritualmuscle. Sam Yun talks about transformation and the Christian journey. Our walk with Christ meets us where we are and moves us to become "who God intends us to be."

After the video has completed, ask the group the following questions and invite discussion:

- Do you feel God nudging you to try something new and do something you haven't done before?
- What are some opportunities God has presented to you?
- What are some challenges to accepting those opportunities?

Reflections (10 minutes) "Letter to God"

Pass out the writing paper, writing utensils, and envelopes.

Say something like:

> "Thank you for that excellent discussion. Now, based on what we've talked about so far, you are invited to write a letter to God. I will write one as well. These letters will not be read by any person except you. After you have finished writing, take an envelope and put your letter inside.

Seal the envelope and write your name on it. I will take the letters to our pastor (staff team, or other group in the church) to pray over during the next six weeks. You will get your letter back at the end of our group's time together.

"Write about what you'd like to experience or learn in the next six weeks. What are your goals? What questions do you have for God? Here are some questions to consider, if you need more writing prompts:

- If you had an opportunity to say anything to God, what would it be?
- What do you want to share with God about the past and the future?
- Is there anything you want to ask—forgiveness? affirmation? acceptance?
- What would be your commitment to God while this group meets?"

Motivate (5 minutes) "God Is Calling You"

Using the computer/TV/screen and internet connection, watch Motivation Clip 1 (available at https://umcyoungpeople.org/spiritualmuscle). Olu Brown reminds us that we are all called to be disciples of Christ. We must hear the call and accept it as the first step to our transformation.

Closing

Collect the envelopes if you have not already. Remind the group that they are at the beginning of a journey and shared time together. Say something like:

> God is calling out to us, and we respond by getting to know God. One place we can start to know God is scripture. We can always be connected to God through worship, prayer, and studying the Bible.

Encourage the group to think of getting to know God better through their commitments to read scripture this week. Remind them to do their spiritual workouts, use their journals, and be in prayer for one another until the next meeting. Close with a brief prayer, either by the trainer or the youth.

Spiritual Workout "Word of God" (In *FaithMinder Journals*)

Part of becoming a disciple of Jesus Christ means getting to know Jesus Christ. The Bible reveals details about the person of Jesus Christ to us. Studying the Bible helps us better understand ourselves and our relationship to God. The Bible helps us see God's vision for our lives. Set a goal this week to read from the Gospel of Luke. Read at least four chapters each day for a week. Reflect on the life of Jesus. How can you be more like Christ?

Exploring: Read one chapter a day using these suggestions as a guide: Luke 2, 4, 5, 6, 10, 18, 19.

Following: Read two chapters a day using these suggestions as a guide: Luke 2, 3, 4, 5, 6, 7, 8, 9, 10, 11, 17, 18, 19, 24.

Leading: Read four chapters a day, the whole book of Luke, chapters 1–24.

Go On Moment (In *FaithMinder Journals*)

"God says if you are a disciple of mine, then it means that you must always be on the move. You must always be going; you can't get stuck where you are. You can't stay where you are."—Rev. Olu Brown

Week 1: Believe God

COACH'S PLAYBOOK

Supplies

Bible
FaithMinder Journal
Week 1 videos and something to play them on

Your team is just starting off and may not know what they are getting themselves in to. Make sure that team members have (or get) their *FaithMinder Journals* before the videos this week. Remember, Coach, you see the big picture. You know how these youth want to grow. You get to guide that process and help them do just that. Read 1 Corinthians 9 to prepare yourself!

Foundation

Don't you know that all the runners in the stadium run, but only one gets the prize? So run to win. Everyone who competes practices self-discipline in everything. The runners do this to get a crown of leaves that shrivel up and die, but we do it to receive a crown that never dies. So now this is how I run—not without a clear goal in sight. I fight like a boxer in the ring, not like someone who is shadowboxing. Rather, I'm landing punches on my own body and subduing it like a slave. I do this to be sure that I myself won't be disqualified after preaching to others. (1 Corinthians 9:24-27)

Reflections "Letter to God"

Youth should write in the *FaithMinder Journals* for ten to fifteen minutes. Questions they can consider:

- If you had an opportunity to say anything to God, what would it be?
- What do you want to share with God about the past and the future?
- Would you ask for forgiveness, affirmation, or acceptance?
- What would be your commitment to God?

Youth can share content of their letters with one another or the coach (or not). Journals can be prayed over, or not.

Inspire Video Clip "Here to There"

Watch Inspire Clip 1 (available at https://umcyoungpeople.org/spiritualmuscle). Sam Yun talks about transformation and the Christian journey. Our walk with Christ meets us where we are and moves us to become "who God intends us to be."

Coach's Questions:

- Do you feel God nudging you to try something new and do something you haven't done before?
- What are some opportunities God has presented to you?
- What are some challenges to accepting those opportunities?

Motivate "God Is Calling You"

Using the computer/TV/screen and internet connection, watch Motivation Clip 1 (available at https://umcyoungpeople.org/spiritualmuscle). Olu Brown reminds us that we are all called to be disciples of Christ. We must hear the call and accept it as the first step to our transformation.

Spiritual Workout "Word of God" (In *FaithMinder Journals*)

Part of becoming a disciple of Jesus Christ means getting to know Jesus Christ. The Bible reveals details about the person of Jesus Christ to us. Studying the Bible helps us better understand ourselves and our relationship to God. The Bible helps us see God's vision for our lives. Set a goal this week to read from the Gospel of Luke. Read at least four chapters each day for a week. Reflect on the life of Jesus. How can you be more like Christ?

Go On Moment (In *FaithMinder Journals*)

"God says if you are a disciple of mine, then it means that you must always be on the move. You must always be going; you can't get stuck where you are. You can't stay where you are."—Rev. Olu Brown

Week 2: Mastering Determination

TRAINER'S SCRIPT

Supplies

Bible
FaithMinder Journal
Internet access and computer

Hopefully, youth will have completed their first week of reading in the Gospel of Luke. Be sure to praise their efforts, listen to their challenges, and support them to live into their learning.

Today's scripture speaks to the power of friendship in our lives when we are seeking Christ. You are a significant part of creating friendships and community as youth find out who Jesus is and what he will mean in their lives. Friends, along with determination, can help us find purpose and calling. When did you first hear your calling? When did you first encounter Christ?

Being a follower of Jesus means enduring obstacles and challenges in our Christian journey. Our love of God propels us to keep moving even when things aren't going as we planned or expected. No matter the situation, never lose sight of God's divine plan for us, which is to live a life of joy and peace. Read Romans 8:31-39 and Ecclesiastes, chapter 3, to prepare.

Week 2: Mastering Determination

—◀ TRAINER'S SCRIPT ▶—

Welcome (10 minutes)

Welcome the group. Offer any youth the chance to lead introductions. If there are no volunteers, you go first and direct the order in the group. Share:

- Name
- The most difficult thing about reading the Gospel of Luke last week
- The most interesting thing about reading the Gospel of Luke last week
- A question or learning you got from doing the reading last week

After everyone has introduced themselves and shared, say something like:

"Life is full of ups and downs that challenge us and wear us out. Our goals and determination are what propel us forward. With commitment and diligence, we face any challenges to our faith head-on. God empowers us in our regular practices. We are strong because of God's work in us. We are strong because of God's action and presence in how we practice our faith. We, and God, are determined to grow toward wholeness. That determination comes from our faith itself and our relationship with God, as we prioritize our lives around the love of God and love of neighbor.

"Putting God and God's will for our lives in focus keeps us on the path toward an everlasting life in the Kingdom of God. Today, we'll explore the connection between determination and strength. God is good and provides. God offers grace freely when we stumble. Those who love the Lord can work together, and God is always with us."

Foundation (15 minutes)

Read (or have a youth read) the scripture:

> After a few days, Jesus went back to Capernaum, and people heard that he was at home. So many gathered that there was no longer space, not even near the door. Jesus was speaking the word to them. Some people arrived, and four of them were bringing to him a man who was paralyzed. They couldn't carry him through the crowd, so they tore off part of the roof above where Jesus was. When they had made an opening, they lowered the mat on which the paralyzed man was lying. When Jesus saw their faith, he said to the paralytic, "Child, your sins are forgiven!"
>
> Some legal experts were sitting there, muttering among themselves, "Why does he speak this way? He's insulting God. Only the one God can forgive sins."
>
> Jesus immediately recognized what they were discussing, and he said to them, "Why do you fill your minds with these questions? Which is easier—to say to a paralyzed person, 'Your sins are forgiven,' or to say, 'Get up, take up your bed, and walk'? But so you will know that the Human One has authority on the earth to forgive sins"—he said to the man who was paralyzed, "Get up, take your mat, and go home." (Mark 2:1-11)

Ask two or three of the following questions:

Exploring

- What do you think the friends thought when they saw such a big crowd around Jesus?
- What stories from the Gospel of Luke might have inspired this group to bring their paralyzed friend to Jesus?
- What do you think the paralyzed man was thinking on the way to the house?
  - On the roof?
  - While being lowered toward Jesus?
- Can you think of sins that "paralyze" people today?

Following

- Who had the stronger belief—the paralyzed man or his friends?
- What are Jesus' most popular messages that people "crowd around"?
- What have you done to try to get yourself closer to Jesus?
- What have you done to try to get a friend closer to Jesus?
- Do you think that people need to receive forgiveness before they can be themselves?

Leading

- What does it mean for God to forgive? How can we live out that same spirit of forgiveness and grace?
- What do you think the paralyzed man and his friends talked about on the way home?
- What things crowd out our opportunities to get close with Jesus? How about for our friends' opportunities? What about our enemies' opportunities?
- What authority does a Christian need to give Jesus (and God) in his or her personal life?

Reflections (10 minutes) "God Moves"

Make sure that paper/journals/writing utensils are available. Say something like:

> "Friends can help us push through crowds, challenges, and clutter that separate us from knowing Jesus. The story we just read is of a very personal encounter with Jesus. We know that God also calls to us and moves in our communities quietly at times. We can choose to put ourselves in places where we can more easily hear God. We can also get surprised by God in unlikely places."

Have participants draw, write, or reflect upon the following questions:

- Describe a time or circumstance when you felt God moving in your life.
- How did you know it was God?
- How does scripture confirm or support your experience as an experience from God?
- How is your experience similar to an experience someone else had with God either in the Bible or in the history of the church?
- In what ways in your life do you feel God's presence the most?
- How was your life changed because of God's presence?
- How did you (or have you) shown gratitude for that presence?

Inspire (10 minutes) "I Want More"

Watch Inspire Clip 2 at https://umcyoungpeople.org/spiritualmuscle. Sam Yun reminds us that God is more than our current situation. God wants the best for us, knowing we are part of a broken world. God wants us to live a more purposeful and more abundant life. We must always strive to want more than physical comfort. We are called to discover spiritual things that truly sustain us.

After the video has completed, ask the groups the following questions and invite discussion:

- What are some distractions that keep us from putting or keeping God first in our lives?

- What are some ways that we can be supportive and accountable to one another as we strive to keep on track?
- How does gratitude help us look beyond our circumstances and toward God's promises?

Motivate (5 minutes) "Push Through and Don't Give Up"

Watch Motivation Clip 2 (available at https://umcyoungpeople.org/spiritualmuscle). Taylor Ogden Thomas talks about the obstacles that can get in the way of our getting closer to Jesus. No matter what tries to block us from our blessing, we must keep pushing. With the help of our friends, we can stay focused and move past the stuff that interferes with our relationship with God and Jesus. True power comes from connection.

Closing

Say something like:

> "We are covered by God's grace no matter where we are in our journey. We are surrounded by grace. We can show grace to our friends and find strength in community. There will always be challenges and hurdles to jump over as we run the race. But we should realize that it is in cooperation, not competition, that we discover who we are in Christ Jesus."

Encourage youth to reflect on their own hurdles and their friends and to appreciate the community around them this coming week. If youth do not feel that they are surrounded by grace or a community, take extra time to talk with them. Offer new and different chances to connect in the church, or ask why they don't feel surrounded by grace. Yes, God's grace is truly sufficient and is overflowing beyond our comprehension. We should always be thankful and encouraged that God is always working in our favor.

Spiritual Workout "Grace and Gratitude" (In *FaithMinder Journals*)

There is no greater way to worship God than with our thanks and praise. We come to God during the hard times, and we come to God in the good times, too. Set a goal this week to explore your community and friendships. Find ways that you can show thanks and gratitude for what surrounds you.

Exploring: Choose two days this week to walk around your community (in safe locations and at a safe time, of course). Take at least thirty minutes, and look for specifics and details that you would call "beautiful." Find a park, an intersection, or some other place that feels sacred or special. Take a photograph, draw a picture, or write down what makes those places feel special. Say a prayer thanking God for unexpected beauty around you. Talk with friends about any speed bumps or challenges that are making life hard for them right now. Ask if there is anything you can do to help them.

Following: Choose two days this week to walk around your community (in safe locations and at a safe time, of course). Take at least thirty minutes and look for specifics and details that you find beautiful. Find a park, an intersection, or some other place that feels sacred or special. Take a photograph, draw a picture, or write down what makes those places feel special. Say a prayer thanking God for unexpected beauty around you. Meet with a group of friends (Christian or not) and talk about speed bumps or challenges that are making life tough. Ask if there is anything you can do to help, and offer to pray for them. You can pray out loud with them or silently later on.

Leading: Choose three days this week to walk around your community (in safe locations and at a safe time, of course). Take at least thirty minutes, and look for specifics and details that you find beautiful. Find a park, an intersection, or some other place that feels sacred or special. Take a photograph, draw a picture, or write down what makes those places feel special. Say a prayer thanking God for unexpected beauty around you. Meet with a group of friends (Christian or not) and talk about speed bumps or challenges that are making life tough. Ask if there is anything you can do to help, and offer to pray for them. You can pray out loud with them or silently later on. Reflect upon ways that you could act like the friends of the paralyzed man in Mark 2. Write in your journal about ways that you could bring others to know Jesus or get to know God.

Go On Moment (In *FaithMinder Journals*)

"Because of God's mercy we have work to do. He has given it to us, and we must not give up."—Taylor Ogden Thomas

Week 2: Mastering Determination

COACH'S PLAYBOOK

Supplies

Bible
FaithMinder Journal
Internet access and computer

Life is full of ups and downs. No matter what life throws at us, we must constantly move forward with commitment and diligence. Anchored in faith, we can determine the priorities in our lives and put God first. Putting God first and paying attention to God's will keeps our focus on the finish line–an everlasting life as part of the Kingdom of God. Stay strong and remember God is good and provides. Those who love the Lord can find harmony in chaos. God is always with us.

Being a follower of Jesus means enduring obstacles and challenges in our Christian journey. It will take determination to overcome. Our love of God propels us to keep moving even when things do not go according to our plans. No matter the situation, never lose sight of God's divine hope for us: to live a life of joy and peace in connection with one another and God. Read Romans 8:31-39 and Ecclesiastes, chapter 3, to prepare.

Foundation (15 minutes)

After a few days, Jesus went back to Capernaum, and people heard that he was at home. So many gathered that there was no longer space, not even near the door. Jesus was speaking the word to them. Some people arrived, and four of them were bringing to him a man who was paralyzed. They couldn't carry him through the crowd, so they tore off part of the roof above where Jesus was. When they had made an opening, they lowered the mat on which the paralyzed man was lying. When Jesus saw their faith, he said to the paralytic, "Child, your sins are forgiven!"

Some legal experts were sitting there, muttering among themselves, "Why does he speak this way? He's insulting God. Only the one God can forgive sins."

Jesus immediately recognized what they were discussing, and he said to them, "Why do you fill your minds with these questions? Which is easier—to say to a paralyzed person, 'Your sins are forgiven,' or to say, 'Get up, take up your bed, and walk'? But so you will know that the Human One has authority on the earth to forgive sins"—he said to the man who was paralyzed, "Get up, take your mat, and go home." (Mark 2:1-11)

Reflections "God Moves"

Youth should write in the *FaithMinder Journals* for ten to fifteen minutes. Questions they can consider:

- Describe a time or circumstance where you felt God moving in your life.
- How did you know it was God?
- In what ways in your life do you feel God's presence the most?
- How was your life changed because of God's presence?
- How did you show (or have you shown) gratitude for that presence?

Inspire "I Want More"

Watch Inspire Clip 2 (available at https://umcyoungpeople.org/spiritualmuscle). Sam Yun reminds us that God is more than our current situation. God wants the best for us, knowing we are part of a broken world. God wants us to live a more purposeful and more abundant life. We must always strive to want more than physical comfort. We are called to discover spiritual things that truly sustain us.

Coach's Questions

- What are some distractions that prevent us from keeping God first in our lives?
- How can we be supportive and accountable to one another as we strive to keep on track?
- How does gratitude help us look beyond our circumstances and toward God's promises?

Motivate "Push Through and Don't Give Up"

Watch Motivation Clip 2 (available at https://umcyoungpeople.org/spiritualmuscle). Taylor Ogden Thomas talks about the obstacles that can get in our way of our getting closer to Jesus. No matter what tries to block us from our blessing, we must keep pushing. With the help of our friends, we can stay focused and move past the stuff that interferes with our relationship with God and Jesus. True power comes from connection.

Spiritual Workout "Grace and Gratitude" (In *FaithMinder Journals*)

There is no greater way to worship God than with our thanks and praise. We come to God during the hard times, and we come to God in the good times too. Set a goal this week to explore your community and friendships. Find ways that you can show thanks and gratitude for what surrounds you.

Choose three days this week to walk around your community (in safe locations and at a safe time, of course). Take at least thirty minutes and look for specifics and details that you find beautiful. Discover a park, an intersection, or some other place that feels sacred or unique. Take a photograph, draw a picture, or write down what makes those places feel special. Say a prayer thanking God for unexpected beauty around you. Meet with a group of friends (Christian or not) and talk about speed bumps or challenges that are making life tough. Ask if there is anything you can do to help, and offer to pray for them. You can pray out loud with them or silently later on. Reflect upon ways that you could act like the friends of the paralyzed man in Mark 2. Write in your journal about ways that you could bring others to know Jesus or get to know God.

Go On Moment (In *FaithMinder Journals*)

"Because of God's mercy, we have work to do. He has given it to us, and we must not give up."—Taylor Ogden Thomas

Week 3: Change Is Good

TRAINER'S SCRIPT

Supplies

Bible
FaithMinder Journal
Internet access and computer
Scrap paper, several pieces per person

As we grow in Christ, we must be willing to leave some things behind. God wants us to leave behind negativity because God is a God of hope. When we leave behind negativity, we open ourselves to God's possibilities. What is ahead of us is so much more than what is behind us. Unload what is weighing you down and holding you back to be free and agile for the path before you. Our days are so full of distractions and things that pull us away from our relationship with God. Fear, shame, and doubt can blur our vision and block our line of sight. As a leader, encourage youth not to be like Lot's wife who didn't know how to let go and trust God. Be open to change, allowing yourself to be transformed and find peace, joy, and freedom.

By this week, youth may be experiencing some fatigue, especially as the exercises during the week become more challenging. Inspire them by keeping their focus on the future, what they are growing toward. This week, youth will explore the dynamic between the past and future, those things that weigh down our spirit versus those that lift us up in our spiritual growth. Part of building spiritual muscle is giving up on the things that create distance between us and God. When we discuss fasting, we are not asking youth to give up something they need. Fasting should create some discomfort. In that discomfort, we can discover new ways of connecting with God and create free space and time to act as Christians should. In guiding youth to figure out what they will fast from, make sure they know that whatever they give up should not cause them any harm.

With faith comes action, and the two work together to form us as Christians. We commit to our ongoing spiritual growth, to become the people God intended each of us to be. By doing so, we turn what we believe into an outward display of our faith. By becoming more like Christ, we increase our love for God and our love for one another. The goodness of the Lord leads us to repentance. As youth practice new spiritual disciplines, such as fasting, God will begin to shine a light on behaviors or things that need to be left behind. As God weeds out the bad, youth need to learn about the difference between conviction and condemnation. God's conviction is sweet and invites us to live in a way in which we can better recognize God's goodness. This is very different than condemnation that we can experience. Condemnation comes from judgment. Condemnation leads to shame, disappointment, and feelings of not being good enough. Ensure that youth know that they are good enough and God loves them!

Guide the discussion to bring up issues and situations that shackle us spiritually. Examine how we can simplify our lives, let go of the past, and clear the way for God to enter. Read Ephesians, chapter 4, to prepare.

Week 3: Change Is Good

TRAINER'S SCRIPT

Welcome (10 minutes)

Welcome the group. Offer youth the chance to lead introductions. If there are no volunteers, you go first and direct the order in the group. Share:

- Name
- A sacred or special place that you found last week in your community
- One thing that you heard a friend (or friends) struggling with

After everyone has checked in, say something like:

"Thank you all for sharing and keeping up with your activities during the week. I am often reminded of the love of God when we are together. I am reminded of the disciples and Jesus in the questions that we ask and raise. Some of the things that your friends (and maybe us, too!) struggle with are things that hold us back from maturing, or growing up, in Christ. Today, we are going to explore change. What does it mean to leave things behind as a part of growing up? We'll talk about things we can put away as we try to become mature Christians.

"Growing up in Christ doesn't mean just becoming old enough to look like an adult; it means discovering who we are as a part of God's family. Sometimes, growing up (becoming mature) can be painful. Growing pains happen physically to our bodies, and we'll experience those as our faith stretches us to think and act in new ways. Luckily, growing up in Christ doesn't mean becoming perfect either. John Wesley, the founder of the Methodist movement, preached that we were all 'on the journey toward perfection.' Let's pause here, because this is important. When we use words like *perfect* or *perfection,* we don't mean that we can become people who will never sin or do wrong. The Wesleyan idea of Christian perfection is more like becoming complete, whole, or mature in faith. The idea is that we can become complete in our love for God and our love for one another. That completeness gets worked out in our actions and in the state of our hearts. So don't get hung up on the word *perfect.* Instead, think about wholeness, completeness, and maturity. Paul the Apostle (who wrote a lot of the New Testament) recognized that he wasn't complete, but he could grow toward a more complete understanding of God, Christ, and the Holy Spirit by changing his actions."

Foundation (15 minutes)

Read (or have a youth read) the following scripture:

> The righteousness that I have comes from knowing Christ, the power of his resurrection, and the participation in his sufferings. It includes being conformed to his death so that I may perhaps reach the goal of the resurrection of the dead. It's not that I have already reached this goal or have already been perfected, but I pursue it, so that I may grab hold of it because Christ grabbed hold of me for just this purpose. Brothers and sisters, I myself don't think I've reached it, but I do this one thing: I forget about the things behind me and reach out for the things ahead of me. The goal I pursue is the prize of God's upward call in Christ Jesus. (Philippians 3:10-14)

Ask a two or three of the following questions:

Exploring

- Growing up, was there an art, skill, or sport you wanted to get better at by practicing? Were you able to practice enough to recognize improvement?
- Describe the characteristics of someone with a mature faith.
- Do you think Jesus was perfect? Why or why not?
- What is something that you own that you value? Could you live without that thing for an hour? day? week? month?

Following

- What was something you did as a younger child that you don't do anymore?
- Is there anything you did as a younger child that you still do?
- What behaviors can get left behind when trying to be Christian?

- Think of a person who is hard for you to deal with in life. How might your attitude or actions change toward that person as you grow in love for God and others?
- Are there things you want to stop doing or leave behind because of your faith?
- What do you think Paul means by "being conformed to his (Jesus') death"?
- Do you think that forgetting about things behind you and reaching out for what is ahead is good advice from Paul? Why or why not?

Leading

- What does Paul mean by "pursuing the prize of God's upward call"?
- Have you noticed a difference in how you act as a Christian versus before you knew about Jesus or committed to be a disciple?
- What is one way God is increasing love in you for God or for others?
- Jesus dies, is resurrected, and that promise of new life is given to Christians as well. What is God calling you to reach out for? What is ahead of you with your life in Christ?

Inspire (15 Minutes) "Rise Up"

Say something like:

> "The story of Christ ends *and* begins with his death and resurrection. We don't literally have to die to follow Christ. However, following Christ does mean that we put some things down in order to find new life in Christ. Choosing what we put down—what parts of ourselves we let die—is an important part of growing up in Christ. The truth is we become who God intended us to be in the very beginning, when we give ourselves to God's transforming love. We become more of ourselves than ever before when God rids us of sin and matures us in love."

Watch Inspire Clip 3 (available at https://umcyoungpeople.org/spiritualmuscle). Sam Yun uncovers the notion of dying with Christ and then rising again to live with Christ. He shares Paul's journey and how a persecutor of Jesus became one of the greatest evangelists of all time.

After the video has completed, ask the group the following questions and invite discussion:

- How do the feelings of fear and shame hold us back from being the disciples that Christ wants us to be?
- How can our own personal transformation (changes) create transformation (change) in our faith community (church)?
- How can our lives be a testimony to help others on their journey?

Reflections (10 Minutes) "Look To Jesus"

Say something like:

"Paul was so moved by Jesus that he let go of his own agenda, bad habits, and hard heart, and he allowed God to transform him for good works. He didn't allow his past to dictate his future. He was willing to be open to being a follower of Christ and sharing his message with the world. Paul didn't lose himself—he actually became more fully himself when he allowed God to weed out the sin and transform him for God's mission in the world. Let's take some journal time. I will ask you to be open to the ideas that Jesus calls us to new life, to become the best version of ourselves that we can be. Invite God's presence as you write, and watch God do amazing things though you.

"I'll give you several questions to respond to. Write, draw, or do whatever invites God's presence into your mind.

- Describe the moment (or moments) when you decided to follow Jesus.
- How has knowing Jesus changed you or is currently changing you?
- What are some things you had to leave behind to grow up and go forward in Christ?
- What has been added to your life because of your faith?"

Motivate (5 Minutes) "Mountain of Stuff"

As youth finish writing in their journals, watch Motivation Clip 3 at https://umcyoungpeople.org/spiritual muscle. Cedrick Bridgeforth challenges us to get rid of all the mountains of stuff that block our path on our journey. We often fill our lives with things that are not important and actually drain us of our energy and resources. Cedrick encourages us to make room for the "saving things" that bring purpose and direction toward everlasting life.

Closing (5 minutes)

Pass out the scrap paper, giving each student several pieces. Say something like:

"You heard Cedrick talk about the mountains of stuff we carry around. You heard about the transformation Paul went through and some of what inspired him to write about forgetting the things that were behind him and focusing on what is ahead. Take a minute or two and on each scrap of paper, write something that is holding back your ability to connect with God and live like Jesus. Write as little or as much as you want. When you have finished writing, scrunch up the paper into a little ball. While you wad up the paper, say a prayer to yourself for strength to focus on what lies ahead and not what is behind. Leave your scrunched up paper in a pile by me before you go. We'll make our own little mountain of stuff that we can leave behind."

Remind the students to do their spiritual workouts for the week.

Spiritual Workout "Simplify Your Life"

Fasting demonstrates our ability to let go of unimportant things so that we lean on God more. When we let go of the things that hold us back, we free up our lives. That freedom creates space for God's blessings in our lives. What things hold us back from deeply connecting with God? Maybe some fun things. Spending money on wants (dining out, expensive clothes, etc.) or partying (along with drinking or using drugs) might be examples. Fasting means letting go of some serious things as well—giving up anger or letting go of a grudge, for example. God doesn't want you to give up all the fun stuff of life. Instead, God invites you to experience life in a community as your authentic self. Fasting helps us appreciate what we already have. Biblical fasts always involved food and consumption.

Pick something that you care about but that you could give up in the coming week. Where do you spend time, energy, or money in ways that distract you from your faith life? Consider fasting from technology (reduce your screen time with TVs, smartphones, etc.). Consider fasting from gossip, spreading rumors, or saying things that hurt others. Consider fasting from soft drinks, candy, or unhealthy foods. Consider fasting from the "wants" that you spend money on. Consider the emotional energy you spend on drama in friendships. Replace the time, space, and energy that you give up with a spiritual practice. Commit to a daily devotion or volunteer your time when you would normally be watching a show. Instead of eating out at a restaurant or going to a coffee shop, take what you would have spent and donate it to a local ministry. Instead of gossiping, maybe start a daily noon prayer time or a prayer text circle with your friends. Be creative in what you fast *from* and what you *will do* instead!

Exploring

Think of one thing that you spend a lot of time, money, or energy on that you could give up for the week. Commit to fasting three days this week. Instead of doing that one thing, read Isaiah 58:3-7 and pray that, by fasting from your one thing, you will continue to create space for God in your life. Pray to keep your focus on what is ahead instead of behind. Write about your experiences in your journal.

Following

Think of one thing that you spend a lot of time, money, or energy on that you could give up for the week. Commit to fasting six days this week. Instead of doing that one thing, read Matthew 6:16-18, Isaiah

58:3-7, and Luke 18:1-12. Find an opportunity to pray with a group of friends during the week. Pray that by fasting from your one thing you will continue to create space for God in your life; pray that, by fasting, you can overcome unexpected addictions and that God will notice your fast, even if people do not. Pray to keep your focus on what is ahead instead of behind. Write about your experiences in your journal.

Leading

Think of one thing that you spend a lot of time, money, or energy on that you could give up for the week. Commit to fasting every day this week. Instead of doing that one thing, Read 2 Samuel 12:15-17, Psalm 35, Matthew 6:16-18, Isaiah 58:3-7, and Luke 18:1-12. Find ways to volunteer, serve others, and give money during the week. Pray that, by fasting from your one thing, you will continue to create space for God in your life. Pray that through fasting, God will intervene on your behalf, fasting will keep you humble as a Christian, God will see your fast, and any addictions may come to light. Pray to keep your focus on what is ahead instead of behind. Write about your experiences in your journal.

**A note on fasting. Fasting is meant as a spiritual exercise. It should not cause harm to your body. If you are considering a biblical fast or other fast that involves giving up food or drink for periods of time, discuss this with trusted adults or healthcare providers. Your spiritual muscles won't be stronger if your body is weak from excessive fasting!*

Go On Moment (In *FaithMinder Journals*)

"You are not what you do. You are not what you have. You are not what others say about you."—Cedrick Bridgeforth

Week 3: Change Is Good

COACH'S PLAYBOOK

Supplies

Bible
FaithMinder Journal
Internet access and computer

As we grow in Christ, we must be willing to leave some things behind. What awaits us in Christ means so much more than things in the past. Unload what weighs you down and holds you back. Be free and agile to follow the path before you. Our days are so full of distractions and things that pull us away from our relationship with God. Fear, shame, and doubt can blur our vision and block our line of sight. Let us not be like Lot's wife who didn't know how to let go and trust God. Allow yourself to be transformed to find peace, joy, and freedom.

With faith comes action; the two work together to form us as Christians. We must commit to our ongoing spiritual growth, to become better people, and to turn what we believe into an outward display of our faith. Guide the discussion to bring up issues and situations that shackle us spiritually. Examine how we can simplify our lives, let go of the past, and clear the way for God to enter. Read Ephesians, chapter 4, to prepare.

Foundation

> The righteousness that I have comes from knowing Christ, the power of his resurrection, and the participation in his sufferings. It includes being conformed to his death so that I may perhaps reach the goal of the resurrection of the dead. It's not that I have already reached this goal or have already been perfected, but I pursue it, so that I may grab hold of it because Christ grabbed hold of me for just this purpose. Brothers and sisters, I myself don't think I've reached it, but I do this one thing: I forget about the things behind me and reach out for the things ahead of me. The goal I pursue is the prize of God's upward call in Christ Jesus. (Philippians 3:10-14)

Reflections "Look to Jesus"

Youth should write in the *FaithMinder Journals* for ten to fifteen minutes. Questions they can consider:

- Describe the moment (or moments) when you decided to follow Jesus and become a Christian.
- How has knowing Jesus changed you or is currently changing you?
- What are some things you had to leave behind to grow up and go forward in Christ?
- What has been added to your life because of your faith?

Inspire "Rise Up"

Watch Inspire Clip 3 at https://umcyoungpeople.org/about/building-spiritual-muscle-videos. Sam Yun uncovers the notion of dying with Christ and then rising again to live with Christ. He shares Paul's journey about how a persecutor of Jesus became one of the greatest evangelists of all time.

Coach's Questions:

- How do the feelings of fear and shame hold us back from being the disciples that Christ wants us to be?
- How can our own personal transformation (changes) create transformation (change) in our faith community [church]?
- How can our lives be a testimony to help others on their journey?

Motivate (5 Minutes) "Mountain of Stuff"

As youth finish writing in their journals, watch Motivation Clip 3 at https://umcyoungpeople.org/spiritualmuscle. Cedrick Bridgeforth challenges us to get rid of all the "mountains of stuff" that block our path on our journey. We often fill our lives with things that are not important and actually drain us of our energy and resources. Cedrick encourages us to make room for the "saving things" that bring purpose and direction toward everlasting life.

Spiritual Workout "Simplify Your Life"

Fasting demonstrates our ability to let go of unimportant things so that we lean on God more. When we let go of the things that hold us back, we free up our lives. That freedom creates space for God's blessings in our lives. What things hold us back from deeply connecting with God? Maybe some fun things. Spending money on wants (dining out, expensive clothes, etc.) or partying (along with drinking or using drugs) might be examples. Fasting means letting go of some serious things as well—Giving up anger or holding on to a grudge, for example. God doesn't want you to give up all the fun stuff of life. Instead, God invites you to experience life in a community as your authentic self. Fasting helps us appreciate what we already have. Biblical fasts always involved food and consumption.

Pick something that you care about, but could give up in the coming week. Where do you spend time, energy, or money in ways that distract you from your faith life? Consider fasting from technology (reduce your screen time with TVs, smartphones, etc.). Consider fasting from gossip, spreading rumors, or saying things that hurt others. Consider fasting from soft drinks, candy, or unhealthy foods. Consider fasting from the "wants" that you spend money on. Consider the emotional energy you spend on drama in friendships. Replace the time, space, and energy that you give up with a spiritual practice. Commit to a daily devotion or volunteer your time when you would normally be watching a show. Instead of eating out at a restaurant or going to a coffee shop, take what you would have spent and donate it to a local ministry. Instead of gossiping, maybe start a daily noon prayer time or a prayer text circle with your friends. Be creative in what you fast *from* and what you *will do* instead!

**A note on fasting. Fasting is meant as a spiritual exercise. It should not cause harm to your body. If you are considering a biblical fast or other fast that involves giving up food or drink for periods of time, discuss with trusted adults or healthcare providers. Your spiritual muscles won't be stronger if your body is weak from excessive fasting!*

Go On Moment (In *FaithMinder Journals*)

"You are not what you do. You are not what you have. You are not what others say about you."—Cedrick Bridgeforth

Week 4: Proceed with Passion

—TRAINER'S SCRIPT—

Supplies

Bible
FaithMinder Journal
Internet access and computer
Spiritual Gifts Survey (http://www.umc.org/what-we-believe/spiritual-gifts-online-assessment)
Things that create light or warmth (matches, a lighter, candles, etc.)
A picture of the United Methodist cross and flame

The image of the cross and flame representing The United Methodist Church is a symbol of the Evangelical United Brethren and Methodist Churches joining together. It could also be a symbol of the fire and passion within each of us as followers of Christ. When we bring our spiritual passions and God-given gifts together, we shine! God created us with purpose. Transformation in our lives results in our living out our purpose by sharing our gifts with the world. As Christians, we share not out of obligation or ritual but because God first loved us. Love is our natural response to God's love. Spiritual passion is more than a feeling; it is our excitement for serving God that moves us to action! Our gifts should shine as a bright light in a dark place. That light will transform us and transform the world.

Help participants think this coming week about how their gifts connect to their lives at work, school, community, and church. Many youth think that being called to ministry means becoming an ordained pastor or working at a church. However, every Christian is called to ministry. Everyone is called to serve and live out that call. In everything we do, we should use our gifts as an offering to God. As we discover our spiritual gifts, we can strengthen our relationship with God and live in tune with God's will. Read 1 Corinthians 12 to prepare.

Week 4: Proceed with Passion

—◀ TRAINER'S SCRIPT ▶—

Welcome (15 minutes)

Welcome the group. Be the first to introduce yourself and set the tone and order for other introductions. Arrange the things that create warmth/light along with the picture of the UMC cross and flame in the space where you are meeting. Share:

- Name
- What I fasted from last week
- What was meaningful about the fasting or what I added
- One way that an item in the warmth/light pile could create joy

After people have introduced themselves, say something like:

"Thank you for keeping up with the activities during the week. I am sure that you are seeing growth in your spiritual muscle with the exercises you've been doing for the past month! At this point in our time together, we have to keep ourselves motivated for what is ahead. Our motivation can come from recognizing our gifts and finding our passion in Christ. Each of the things we talked about creates warmth, light, and joy in its own way. Our actions as Christians can create warmth, light, and joy as well.

"It can feel complicated to be a Christian sometimes. So many Bible verses, so many questions, so many ways to find God and Jesus. In the Gospel of Luke, Jesus helps simplify many of the laws and rules that were written in the Old Testament. His simplification is often referred to as the Great Commandment. It can be found in Matthew (22:35-40), Mark (12:28-31), Luke

(10:25-28), and John (13:34). As Christians, we are supposed to love God and love our neighbors. As we show love for God and love for neighbor, we can create warmth, light, and joy for ourselves and others."

Foundation (10 minutes)

Read (or have a youth read) the scripture:

> A legal expert stood up to test Jesus. "Teacher," he said, "what must I do to gain eternal life?"
>
> Jesus replied, "What is written in the Law? How do you interpret it?"
>
> He responded, *"You must love the Lord your God with all your heart, with all your being, with all your strength, and with all your mind, and love your neighbor as yourself."*
>
> Jesus said to him, "You have answered correctly. Do this and you will live."
>
> But the legal expert wanted to prove that he was right, so he said to Jesus, "And who is my neighbor?" (Luke 10:25-29)

Ask two or three of the following questions:

Exploring

- What is the legal expert looking for when he asks Jesus his first question?
- What things can you do to show you love for God with your "heart, being, strength, and mind"?
- What does it mean "to love your neighbor as yourself"?
- What do you think the legal expert was passionate about, based on his two questions?
- What do you think Jesus is passionate about in this conversation?

Following

- Why would the legal expert call Jesus "teacher"?
- Why do you think that Jesus answers the legal expert's question with another question?
- How would you answer the question, "Who is my neighbor?"
- How is God changing you as you participate in the spiritual practices we've been doing week to week?
- How are you trying to love your neighbor as yourself?
- How does living out the Great Commandment help you discover your spiritual passions?

Leading

- How does showing your love for God feed your spiritual passions?
- How does showing your love for your neighbor feed your spiritual passions?
- Who are the neighbors that you have been serving as a Christian?
- Are there some neighbors whom you may have missed or overlooked who could use warmth and light?
- Why does the legal expert ask two questions?

Reflections (10 minutes) "Do What You Love"

Say something like:

> "Sometimes religious people are passionate about 'getting it right.' Getting faith right is important, and getting it right means loving God and neighbor. Being in good relationship with God and neighbor by acting like Christ gets it right.
>
> "After the legal expert's second question, Jesus offers up the parable of the good Samaritan. It's a story of religious people who miss the opportunity to serve their neighbor. The legal expert who asks Jesus the questions was passionate about getting it right, and the religious people in the parable also want to get it right, but their focus isn't on God or neighbors. Somehow their focus and passion ended up somewhere else. The parable of the good Samaritan is about being moved to action because of a passion to serve others. Let's take a few moments to reflect on 'getting it right,' our neighbors, and joy. Here are some questions to consider as you write or draw."

- Think of something you do that brings you the most joy.
  - When did you first discover that you enjoyed doing it?
  - What is your first memory of this activity?
- Who is my neighbor?
  - How do I meet my neighbors?
  - What do I think "getting it right" as a Christian means?
- What is God's passion for my life?
  - How am I trying to stay connected to God?
  - How am I learning more about Jesus' life and teachings?
  - How could I use my passions for God and to help my neighbors?
  - By using my passions and gifts, how is God transforming my life?

*Optional—As students write, play "We Must Praise" by J. Moss for the group (https://www.youtube.com/watch?v=NXrUcfcpkrE).

Inspire (10 minutes) "Moved to Action"

Watch Inspire Clip 4 at https://umcyoungpeople.org/spiritualmuscle. Sam Yun dives into the story of the good Samaritan. This parable is an excellent example of a situation moving a person to act. Just as the good Samaritan used his gifts for good, Yun shares how our love of God can ignite us to use our gifts for ministry and service.

After the video has completed, ask the group the following questions and invite discussion:

- What excites you about mission? Share about someone else you know who has helped a person in need. How do you see this act of mercy shaping the person to be more like Christ?
- What are some ways that we can keep from getting comfortable and complacent in our faith? In our worship and our mission?
- How do we share our gifts and abilities to show the love of Christ?

Motivate (5 minutes) "Created for Greatness"

Watch Motivation Clip 4 at https://umcyoungpeople.org/spiritualmuscle. Mike Slaughter moves us to reflect on our lives and our call to ministry. All of us have been created with a purpose. Just as God created all things in the universe, God also created you. The gift of life isn't to be taken lightly. We must tap into our authentic selves, reveal our true purpose, and offer ourselves as our gift back to God.

Closing

Say something like:

> "God wants us to be in community and use our gifts to help others. We are God's gift to the world, and we can provide light for those in darkness, warmth for those who are cold, and joy for those who walk in sadness. Our true purpose is to worship God, understand who Jesus is, and be moved by the Holy Spirit to action. Just as a match gets struck to create warmth and light, what we witness in the world should strike us so that we are moved into action. We can submit ourselves to live the life of a disciple and transform the world."

*If there are specific aspects of your church where youth could serve and connect, share that information. Youth may not realize their gifts can be valuable to the church, especially if they don't know all the ministry opportunities that your church offers!

Spiritual Workout "Mission" (In *FaithMinder Journals*)

The *mission* of the United Methodist Church is to make disciples of Jesus Christ for the transformation of the world. Your local church probably has a mission as well. A *mission* is the goal or purpose of a church or person that guides everything that church or person does.. The word *missions* means something different. *Missions* are opportunities to provide for others. This week, you will explore and understand the mission of your local church. You will also discover missions happening in your church and community.

Pick a day this week to serve others in need. Identify a local church, school, or organization where you can give your time, resources, and talents.

Exploring

Find out the mission of your church. Ask the pastor or other leaders in the church. Find out what missions your church leads or participates in. Make a list and find out whether you could participate in those missions in the future. Identify one missions opportunity from your church or community that would feed your spiritual passions.

Following

Find out the mission of your church. Ask the pastor or other leaders in the church. Find out what missions your church leads or participates in. Make a list, and find out whether you could participate in those missions in the future. Identify one missions opportunity from your church or community that would feed your spiritual passions. Take the spiritual gifts survey (http://www.umc.org/what-we-believe/spiritual-gifts-online-assessment). Write in your journal about how your top three gifts could be used for your church's mission and missions.

Leading

Find out the mission of your church. Ask the pastor or other leaders in the church. Find out what missions your church leads or participates in. Make a list and find out whether you could participate in those missions in the future. Identify one missions opportunity from your church or community that would feed your spiritual passions. Take the spiritual gifts survey (http://www.umc.org/what-we-believe/spiritual-gifts-online-assessment). Write in your journal about how your top three gifts could be used in mission and missions. Compare the missions offered by your church with the needs of your community. If there is a gap, or a need not being met, brainstorm and write down some ideas for how you could use your gifts to meet those needs. Bring your ideas to church leadership, and consider starting a missions opportunity for others to join!

Go On Moment (In *FaithMinder Journals*)

"All of you have a calling; God has created you uniquely with a special purpose."—Mike Slaughter

Week 4: Proceed with Passion

—◀ COACH'S PLAYBOOK ▶—

Supplies

Bible
FaithMinder Journal
Internet access and computer

The image of the cross and flame representing The United Methodist Church is a symbol of the Evangelical United Brethren and Methodist Churches joining together. It could also be a symbol of the fire and passion within each of us, as followers of Christ. When we bring our spiritual passions and God-given gifts together, we shine! God created us with purpose. By sharing our gifts with the world, we live out our purpose. As we share our gifts, we are transformed as the world is transformed. As Christians, we share not out of obligation or ritual, but to show our love for God. Spiritual passion is more than a feeling; it is our excitement for serving God that moves us to action! Our gifts should shine as a bright light in a dark place. That light will transform us and transform the world.

Help participants think this coming week about how their gifts connect to their lives at work, school, community, and church. Many youth think that being called to ministry means becoming an ordained pastor or working at a church. Yet, there are so many ways people can serve and live out their call. In everything we do, we should use our gifts as an offering to God. As we discover our spiritual gifts, we can strengthen our relationship with God and live in tune with God's will. Read 1 Corinthians 12 to prepare.

Foundation

A legal expert stood up to test Jesus. "Teacher," he said, "what must I do to gain eternal life?"

Jesus replied, "What is written in the Law? How do you interpret it?"

He responded, "You must love the Lord your God with all your heart, with all your being, with all your strength, and with all your mind, and love your neighbor as yourself."

Jesus said to him, "You have answered correctly. Do this and you will live."

But the legal expert wanted to prove that he was right, so he said to Jesus, "And who is my neighbor?" (Luke 10:25-29)

Reflections "Do What You Love"

Youth should write in the *FaithMinder Journals* for ten to fifteen minutes. Questions they can consider:

- Think of something you do that brings you the most joy.
  - When did you first discover that you enjoyed doing it?
  - What is your first memory of this activity?
- Who is my neighbor?
  - How do I meet my neighbors?
  - What do I think "getting it right" as a Christian means?
- What is God's passion for my life?
  - How am I trying to stay connected to God?
  - How am I learning more about Jesus' life and teachings?
  - How could I use my passions for God and to help my neighbors?

*Optional—As students write, play "We Must Praise" by J. Moss for the group (https://www.youtube.com/watch?v=NXrUcfcpkrE).

Inspire "Moved to Action"

Watch Inspire Clip 4 at https://umcyoungpeople.org/spiritualmuscle. Sam Yun dives into the story of the good Samaritan. This parable is an excellent example of a situation moving a person to act. Just as the good Samaritan used his gifts for good, Yun shares how our love of God can ignite us to use our gifts for ministry and service.

Coach's Questions:

- What excites you about mission? Share a moment when you, personally, helped someone in need.
- What are some ways that we can keep from getting comfortable and complacent in our faith? In our worship and our mission?
- How do we share our gifts and abilities to show the love of Christ?

Motivate "Created for Greatness"

Watch Motivation Clip 4 at https://umcyoungpeople.org/spiritualmuscle. Mike Slaughter moves us to reflect on our lives and our call to ministry. All of us have been created with a purpose. Just as God created all things in the universe, God also created you. The gift of life isn't to be taken lightly. We must tap into our authentic selves, reveal our true purpose, and offer ourselves as our gift back to God.

Spiritual Workout "Mission" (In *FaithMinder Journals*)

The mission of The United Methodist Church is to make disciples of Jesus Christ for the transformation of the world. Your local church probably has a mission as well. A *mission* is the goal, or purpose, of a church or person that guides everything that church or person does. The word *missions* means something different. Missions are opportunities to provide for others. This week, you will explore and understand the *mission* of your local church. You will also discover *missions* happening in your church and community.

Pick a day this week to serve others in need. Identify a local church, school, or organization where you can give your time, resources, and talents.

Go On Moment (In *FaithMinder Journals*)

"All of you have a calling; God has created you uniquely with a special purpose."—Mike Slaughter

Week 5: Anchored in Discipline

TRAINER'S SCRIPT

Supplies

Bible
FaithMinder Journal
Internet access and computer
Pictures of athletes from different sports, showing different body types

Transformation does not happen in a day or in a single monumental moment in worship. Transformation happens as we invite God into our hearts in every aspect of our lives. God transforms our lives as we transform the muscles in our bodies, with time and diligent repetition of exercise. As we grow stronger into the Word, more mature in our relationship with Christ, and develop endurance in the practice of spiritual disciplines, we strengthen the core spiritual muscles that help us balance our faith and the demands of this world.

We don't just *go* to church–we *are* the church! When we accept Christ into our lives, he becomes a part of who we are and in all that we do. We should fully incorporate our relationship with God and our spiritual strength into our life, community, and relationships. Help the students understand that listening and being obedient to the Holy Spirit is a big part of our discipleship. Read Romans, chapter 8, to prepare.

Week 5: Anchored in Discipline

TRAINER'S SCRIPT

Welcome (10 minutes)

Welcome the group. Be the first to introduce yourself and set the tone and order for other introductions. Make sure that nutritious snacks are available on a table or basket. Be brief and friendly as you share the following information.

- Name
- What you found out about the mission of our church last week
- What missions you discovered and which ones you are interested in serving
- Did you discover a spiritual passion last week? If so, share.

After people have introduced themselves, say something like:

"This past week, you spent some time looking at your own gifts and spiritual passions and a lot of time looking at missions. Missions are how we can serve our church and community, showing our love for our neighbors. Missions by their nature are outward focused.

"This week, we are going to turn our focus inward, toward ourselves. We will find out how ritual and routine can shape and develop our spiritual muscles. Just like your muscles grow and change shape based on the exercises and activities you do, your faith will grow and take shape based on your rituals and routine. One-time exercises don't change our muscles; they just wear them out and leave us stiff and sore. True change happens with discipline."

Inspire (15 minutes) "Instafaith"

Watch Inspire Clip 5 at https://umcyoungpeople.org/spiritualmuscle. Sam Yun visits the Last Supper with Jesus and his disciples, inviting all of us to be a part of a supper that lasts. Ritual and routine can become exercises we use to move from instant faith to deep faith.

After the video has completed, ask the group the following questions and invite discussion:

- What routines do you have in your life, religious or otherwise?
- What do you, personally, get out of going to worship? Other church activities?
- Does Communion, or any other ritual, help provide strength for your daily faith life?
- How can remembering the Last Supper strengthen and unite a church as a body of Christ?

Reflections (10 minutes) "Surrender"

Make sure that the pictures of different athletes are visible to the group. Include traditional and familiar sports (baseball, basketball, soccer, football, etc.) as well as other sports (track, swimming, rock-climbing, parkour, etc.). Strive for diversity in your pictures; include different genders, levels of ability, physical fitness, ethnicities, and so forth.

Say something like:

> "Notice how the muscles in each of these pictures reflect not only their current activity but the preparation for that activity. Someone who is a professional basketball player or Olympic swimmer will typically have more defined muscles than someone playing a pick-up basketball game at the park or someone who goes to a neighborhood swimming pool during the summer. Serious athletes train their bodies with regular exercise. They create exercise routines and spend lots of time preparing for their sport. The body is shaped by the activities it is asked to do. Based on one's choice of sport, the same groups of muscles will develop in different ways. For example, a swimmer will have very different looking shoulder muscles than a tennis player or a sprinter. A cyclist's leg muscles will look very different from those of a basketball player or a weight lifter.
>
> "Our spiritual muscles respond the same way. We can grow a stronger faith by repeating exercises or activities on a regular basis. In church, there are rituals that are repeated. Those rituals can become cornerstones of the routines that we create to build our spiritual muscle. Using our spiritual gifts also builds muscle. Not every person will develop the same amount of strength in the same sets of muscle. That is part of the diversity of gifts in the body of Christ! Take some time to reflect on these questions. Write or draw in your journal for the next ten minutes."

Ask the group the following questions and invite discussion:

- What do you think are the strongest parts of your faith?

- What routines or rituals do you currently do to strengthen your faith?
- Reflect on a time that you felt free.
    - Would you say that your spiritual life helps set you free? Does it provide freedom of movement?
- What does it mean to surrender to God?
- What does God do when I willingly surrender myself to God?

Foundation (15 minutes)

Read (or have a youth read) the scripture:

> You were called to freedom, brothers and sisters; only don't let this freedom be an opportunity to indulge your selfish impulses, but serve each other through love. All the Law has been fulfilled in a single statement: *Love your neighbor as yourself.* But if you bite and devour each other, be careful that you don't get eaten up by each other!
>
> I say be guided by the Spirit and you won't carry out your selfish desires. A person's selfish desires are set against the Spirit, and the Spirit is set against one's selfish desires. They are opposed to each other, so you shouldn't do whatever you want to do. But if you are being led by the Spirit, you aren't under the Law. The actions that are produced by selfish motives are obvious, since they include sexual immorality, moral corruption, doing whatever feels good, idolatry, drug use and casting spells, hate, fighting, obsession, losing your temper, competitive opposition, conflict, selfishness, group rivalry, jealousy, drunkenness, partying, and other things like that. I warn you as I have already warned you, that those who do these kinds of things won't inherit God's kingdom.
>
> But the fruit of the Spirit is love, joy, peace, patience, kindness, goodness, faithfulness, gentleness, and self-control. There is no law against things like this. Those who belong to Christ Jesus have crucified the self with its passions and its desires.
>
> If we live by the Spirit, let's follow the Spirit. Let's not become arrogant, make each other angry, or be jealous of each other. (Galatians 5:13-26)

Ask two or three of the following questions:

Exploring

- Do you think that freedom allows people to be selfish? Why or why not?
- Do you think Paul's list of "selfish actions" is accurate? Would you add or subtract anything from his list?
- Why does Paul use the phrase "fruits of the Spirit"?

- Do you agree or disagree that living out the fruits of the spirit will make you want to live out more fruits of the spirit? Explain why you feel the way you do.
- Do you agree or disagree that doing selfish actions will make you want to do more selfish actions? Explain why you feel as you do.

Following

- The Holy Spirit calls us away from selfish desires. How can being selfish weaken your faith?
- What do you think Paul means when he says "live by the spirit" and that those who belong to Jesus have "crucified the self, along with its passions and desires"?
- How does Communion represent selflessness and the fruits of the spirit?

Leading

- How does having a ritual or routine influence your freedom as a Christian?
- How could you better encourage others to live out the fruits of the spirit?
- Describe what makes Communion meaningful for you.
- What parts of your self have you already set aside to live like Jesus?

Motivate (10 minutes) "I Am the Church"

Say something like:

"The words *disciple* and *discipline* are related; they share the same root word. In Latin, the word *discipulus* means "pupil" or "training." Disciples give themselves up to something or someone else. Christian disciples give themselves up to live a life pleasing to God, modeled in the life of Jesus Christ.

"Discipline can be a routine or a ritual. Discipline is internal motivation that keeps us moving, with the knowledge that we are building strength and endurance in the race God has asked us to run. Practicing spiritual disciplines, like the activities we have been doing since the first week, help keep us connected to God. Discipline helps us receive the direction of the Holy Spirit. Discipline is the difficult 'when-nobody-is-looking' work that we do to prepare us to act like Christians when it really matters. Being a disciple means more than acting like a Christian when we are in trouble or want something; it means we constantly exercise our freedom to build a genuine relationship with Jesus Christ."

Watch Motivation Clip 5 at https://umcyoungpeople.org/spiritualmuscle. Telley Gadson brings a message emphasizing that Jesus and Jesus' power lives in each one of us. She empowers us to think beyond the physical church and the building and inspires us to be the church through our actions.

Closing

Say something like:

> "The exercises we do shape our bodies. The spiritual disciplines we do shape our relationship with God. The church is the body of Christ in the world, and my prayer for each of us this week is that we exercise our freedom selflessly, so that the world can see Christ in you."

Close with a brief prayer, either by the trainer or the youth.

Spiritual Workout "Meditate" (In *FaithMinder Journals*)

Breathing is a great way to slow down and silence distractions of the world. Meditation allows us to commune with God, release stress, and open ourselves to hear God's voice. Prayer and engaging scripture as a part of meditation can help quiet the mind. Use time this week to reflect on or create routines that help you slow your pace and open yourself to God.

Exploring

Meditate for twenty minutes at a time, three days this week. Find a quiet space, no music, no distractions. Just you and God. Breathe slowly. Read the scripture from this week each time you meditate and focus on two questions: (1) "What are the selfish behaviors God wants to get rid of in me?" (2) "Where am I experiencing the fruits of the spirit?" Repeat reading and thinking about those questions until the twenty minutes are up.

Following

Meditate for twenty minutes at a time, five days this week. Find a quiet space, no music, no distractions. Just you and God. Breathe slowly. Use the scriptures from the previous weeks, a different one each time you meditate. Focus on three questions: (1) "What are the selfish behaviors God wants to get rid of in me?" (2) "Where am I experiencing the fruits of the spirit?" (3) "What routines make my faith stronger?" Repeat reading and thinking about those questions until the twenty minutes are up.

Leading

Meditate for thirty minutes at a time, six days this week. Find a quiet space, no music, no distractions—just you and God. Learn about the *Lectio Divina* method for meditating on scripture (http://daily.upperroom.org/?page_id=19). Use the *Audio Lectio* (http://alivenow.upperroom.org/audio-lectio/) for your meditations over your six days. Take one day as a Sabbath break from meditation.

Go On Moment (In *FaithMinder Journals*)

"What Kind of Church Am I? Can Jesus build anything on me?"—Telley Gadson

Week 5: Anchored in Discipline

COACH'S PLAYBOOK

Supplies

Bible
FaithMinder Journal
Internet access and computer

Transformation does not happen in one day or in a single monumental moment in worship. Transformation happens as we invite God into our hearts in every aspect of our lives. We transform our lives just like we transform the muscles in our bodies, with time and diligent repetition of exercise. As we grow stronger into the Word, more mature in our relationship with Christ, and develop endurance in the practice of spiritual disciplines, we strengthen the core spiritual muscles that help us balance our faith and the demands of this world.

We don't just *go* to church–we *are* the church! When we accept Christ into our lives, he becomes a part of who we are and in all that we do. We should fully incorporate our relationship with God and our spiritual strength into our life, community, and relationships. Help the students understand that listening and being obedient to the Holy Spirit is a big part of our discipleship. Read Romans, chapter 8, to prepare.

Foundation

You were called to freedom, brothers and sisters; only don't let this freedom be an opportunity to indulge your selfish impulses, but serve each other through love. All the Law has been fulfilled in a single statement: Love your neighbor as yourself. But if you bite and devour each other, be careful that you don't get eaten up by each other!

I say be guided by the Spirit and you won't carry out your selfish desires. A person's selfish desires are set against the Spirit, and the Spirit is set against one's selfish desires. They are opposed to each other, so you shouldn't do whatever you want to do. But if you are being led by the Spirit, you aren't under the Law. The actions that are produced by selfish motives are obvious, since they include sexual immorality, moral corruption, doing whatever feels good, idolatry, drug use and casting spells, hate, fighting, obsession, losing your temper, competitive opposition, conflict, selfishness, group rivalry, jealousy, drunkenness, partying, and other things like that. I warn you as I have already warned you, that those who do these kinds of things won't inherit God's kingdom.

But the fruit of the Spirit is love, joy, peace, patience, kindness, goodness, faithfulness, gentleness, and self-control. There is no law against things like this. Those who belong to Christ Jesus have crucified the self with its passions and its desires.

If we live by the Spirit, let's follow the Spirit. Let's not become arrogant, make each other angry, or be jealous of each other. (Galatians 5:13-26)

Reflections "Surrender"

Youth should write in the *FaithMinder Journals* for ten to fifteen minutes. Questions they can consider:

- What do you think are the strongest parts of your faith?
- What routines or rituals do you currently do to strengthen your faith?
- Reflect on a time that you felt "free."
    - Would you say that your spiritual life helps set you free? Or does it provide freedom of movement?
- What does it mean to surrender to God?

Inspire "Instafaith"

Watch Inspire Clip 5 at https://umcyoungpeople.org/spiritualmuscle. Sam Yun visits the Last Supper with Jesus and his disciples, inviting all of us to be a part of a supper that lasts. Ritual and routine can become exercises we use to move from instant faith to deep faith.

Coach's Questions:

- What do you think are the strongest parts of your faith?
- What routines or rituals do you currently do to strengthen your faith?
- Reflect on a time that you felt "free."
    - Would you say that your spiritual life helps set you free? Or does it provide freedom of movement?
- What does it mean to surrender to God?

Motivate "I Am the Church"

Watch Motivation Clip 5 at https://umcyoungpeople.org/spiritualmuscle. Telley Gadson brings a message, emphasizing that Jesus and Jesus' power lives in each one of us. She empowers us to think beyond the physical church and the building and inspires us to be the church through our actions.

Spiritual Workout "Meditate" (In *FaithMinder Journals*)

Breathing is a great way to slow down and silence distractions of the world. Meditation allows us to commune with God, release stress, and open ourselves to hear God's voice. Prayer and engaging scripture as a part of meditation can help quiet the mind. Use time this week to reflect on or create routines that help you slow your pace and open yourself to God.

Go On Moment (In *FaithMinder Journals*)

"What Kind of Church Am I? Can Jesus build anything on me?"—Telley Gadson

Week 6: Go On Together

TRAINER'S SCRIPT

Supplies

Bible
FaithMinder Journal
Internet access and computer
Communion elements
Index cards

We are the body of Christ. We can make ourselves strong spiritually, and personal strength translates to a stronger church. We can support one another in love. Lifting one another up builds and strengthens our spiritual muscles. We all have an individual purpose in the Lord, and we have a purpose in community as well. As we go on and train further, we should remember that we do not journey alone. We are a part of a community that loves us, and we can show love to others. Stay in relationship, hold one another accountable, and go on and run the race together! Love God. Love people.

We have come to the end of the six-week study, but it should not be the end of anyone's spiritual journey. We are meant to stay connected and grow together as a community of believers. This week provides a chance for reflection and worship. You already have helped create a safe place for connection, community, and love. For this session, make sure those feelings are present. Following the study, organize a small-group worship service that brings participants together as the body of Christ for Communion and prayer. If you are not able to personally bless the sacraments, invite an ordained elder to be a part of the service. Alternatively, you can have a love feast or agape meal. Read Hebrews 10 to prepare.

Week 6: Go On Together

TRAINER'S SCRIPT

Welcome (10 minutes)

Welcome the group. Be the first to introduce yourself and set the tone and order for other introductions. Make sure that nutritious snacks for the youth are available on a table or basket. Be brief and friendly; share the following information:

- Name
- An experience of meditation from last week

Say something like:

"I am so glad that each of you tried meditation last week. An important part of any training or exercise program is having a variety of activities and also creating chances to rest. If you stretch yourself too thin and make yourself too busy, you might burn out. Instead of generating warmth, light, and joy for others, your energy can get consumed if you forget to take time for yourself. Jesus even liked to find quiet space to pray and meditate. This week, it is time to figure out where to go from here. What spiritual muscles do you want to keep working out? What exercise routine do you want to set for yourself? We've trained together and built endurance for the race ahead. So let's figure out what comes next!"

Inspire (10 minutes) "We are Called"

Watch Inspire Clip 6 at https://umcyoungpeople.org/spiritualmuscle. Sam Yun moves us to continue the journey with the Kingdom as our goal.

God calls everyone. We are called to experience change and transformation. May we stay the course and remember what matters most.

Transition immediately from the video to the scripture.

Foundation (15 minutes)

Read (or have a youth read) the scripture:

> So then let's also run the race that is laid out in front of us, since we have such a great cloud of witnesses surrounding us. Let's throw off any extra baggage, get rid of the sin that trips us up, and fix our eyes on Jesus, faith's pioneer and perfecter. He endured the cross, ignoring the shame, for the sake of the joy that was laid out in front of him, and sat down at the right side of God's throne.
>
> Think about the one who endured such opposition from sinners so that you won't be discouraged and you won't give up. In your struggle against sin, you haven't resisted yet to the point of shedding blood, and you have forgotten the encouragement that addresses you as sons and daughters:
>
> *My child, don't make light of the Lord's discipline*
> *or give up when you are corrected by him,*
> *because the Lord disciplines whomever he loves,*
> *and he punishes every son or daughter whom he accepts.*
>
> Bear hardship for the sake of discipline. God is treating you like sons and daughters! What child isn't disciplined by his or her father? But if you don't experience discipline, which happens to all children, then you are illegitimate and not real sons and daughters. What's more, we had human parents who disciplined us, and we respected them for it. How much more should we submit to the Father of spirits and live? Our human parents disciplined us for a little while, as it seemed best to them, but God does it for our benefit so that we can share his holiness. No discipline is fun while it lasts, but it seems painful at the time. Later, however, it yields the peaceful fruit of righteousness for those who have been trained by it.
>
> So strengthen your drooping hands and weak knees! Make straight paths for your feet so that if any part is lame, it will be healed rather than injured more seriously. Pursue the goal of peace along with everyone—and holiness as well, because no one will see the Lord without it.

Make sure that no one misses out on God's grace. Make sure that no root of bitterness grows up that might cause trouble and pollute many people. (Hebrews 12:1-15)

Ask two or three of the following questions:

Exploring

- What will best encourage you to keep growing in your faith and building spiritual muscle?
- What keeps you from doing the practices that help your spiritual muscles grow?
- What activities that you did to build spiritual muscle were easy for you? Which were difficult for you? Which activities were the most meaningful?
- Tell me about Jesus. Tell me about God.
- What are your next steps with your faith? Where is God calling you?

Following

- Who are "the great cloud of witnesses" that surround you? Who is your community that supports you as you grow in your faith?
- What would you like to learn about the Bible? The church? God? Jesus? The Holy Spirit?
- What spiritual muscles have you exercised the most during our time together?
- How will you continue to pursue the goals of peace and holiness? Where is God calling you?

Leading

- What lifelong disciplines or routines will help your relationship with God through Christ continue to become stronger?
- For whom are you a witness? How are you supporting others in their Christian growth?
- How will you make sure that no one misses out on God's grace in your church? Among your group of friends? In your community?
- How can you lead others and keep "roots of bitterness" from taking root in your community, church, and group of friends?
- Where is God calling you?

Reflections (20 minutes) "Commitment"

Say something like:

> "Obviously we have learned and grown quite a bit in six weeks. Imagine how much more you can grow by keeping up with spiritual exercise! Let's take just a few minutes to write in our journals and on these commitment cards about what you'll keep doing. Use your journal to brainstorm, and use the commitment card to write down one thing that you want us all to know that you'll be working on."
>
> Questions to consider:
>
> - What parts of my faith seem weak, or what are my biggest questions? What exercises would help work out those questions?
> - What parts of my faith are strong and could be used to support others as they grow?
> - How much time per week am I willing to give to continue my intentional discipline?

(In *FaithMinder Journal*) Use this time to make a commitment to yourself, God, and your faith community. After brainstorming ideas and reflecting on your growth in this journal, choose one specific practice to focus on for the next month. Be as specific as possible with your practice; it should continue to build your spiritual muscle and build relationship with God. Write down your commitment on a card, then give the card to the group leader.

After each participant has written his or her commitment card and given it to you, as the trainer, lead your group in *lectio divina* and pray over the cards.

Say something like:

> "An ancient practice of Christian prayer is *lectio divina*, or divine reading. In *lectio divina*, we begin by reading a few verses of the Bible. We read slowly so that we can listen for the message God has for us. We will read the passage several times so that different parts of the reading can grab our attention at different moments.
>
> "As we read, we'll find connections the Spirit reveals between the passage and what is going on in our lives. These are the questions to ask at the beginning of each reading: 'What are you saying to me today, Lord? What am I to hear in this story, parable, or prophecy?' Listening in this way requires patience and a willingness to let go of our own agendas and open ourselves to God's shaping.
>
> "Once we hear a word or phrase that sticks out, your prayer will center on that word or phrase; it is meant for you! From listening, we can move to writing or speaking. We can reflect in anguish, confession, or sorrow; perhaps in joy, praise, thanksgiving, or adoration; perhaps in

anger, confusion, or hurt; perhaps in quiet confidence, trust, or surrender. Finally, after pouring out our heart to God by writing or speaking a prayer, we come to rest simply and deeply in that wonderful, loving presence of God. Reading, reflecting, responding, and resting—this is the basic rhythm of *lectio divina*, divine reading."

Say or print and share these instructions with the youth before reading the scripture for them:

1. Read the scripture slowly. Listen or watch for a key phrase or word that jumps out at you or promises to have special meaning for you. It is better to dwell profoundly on one word or phrase than to skim the surface of several chapters. Read with your own life and choices in mind.
2. Reflect on that key word or phrase. Let it sink into your heart. Align your mind, attention, and emotions in an attitude of reflection. Be like Mary, Jesus' mother, who heard of the angel's announcement and "treasured" and "pondered" what she had heard (Luke 2:19).
3. Respond to what you have read. Form a prayer that expresses your response to the idea, then "pray it back to God." What you have read is woven through what you tell God. You can write, draw, or speak your prayer.
4. Rest in God's word. Let the text soak into your deepest being, savoring an encounter with God and truth. When ready, move toward the moment in which you ask God to show you how to live out what you have experienced.

Read today's scripture for reflection:

> So then let's also run the race that is laid out in front of us, since we have such a great cloud of witnesses surrounding us. Let's throw off any extra baggage, get rid of the sin that trips us up, and fix our eyes on Jesus, faith's pioneer and perfecter. He endured the cross, ignoring the shame, for the sake of the joy that was laid out in front of him, and sat down at the right side of God's throne.
>
> So strengthen your drooping hands and weak knees! Make straight paths for your feet so that if any part is lame, it will be healed rather than injured more seriously. Pursue the goal of peace along with everyone—and holiness as well, because no one will see the Lord without it. Make sure that no one misses out on God's grace. Make sure that no root of bitterness grows up that might cause trouble and pollute many people. (Hebrews 12:1-2, 12-15)

Find out more about *lectio divina* for youth from *DevoZine* (by the Upper Room): http://devozine.upperroom.org/articles/lectio-divina-listening-to-god.

Motivate (5 minutes) "Church on the Move"

Watch Motivation Clip 6 at https://umcyoungpeople.org/spiritualmuscle. Telley Gadson ignites us to be a church on the move. We are not just the things inside the walls, we are to go outside church walls to share the light and love all we encounter.

Spiritual Workout (10 minutes) "Worship and Communion"

Have elements for Communion or a love feast ready. Place the commitment cards by the Communion elements.

Say something like: "We will close our time together with Communion, the ancient practice that ties us to Jesus' earliest disciples. Your commitment cards are next to the elements, because we wish to bless those efforts as well as the elements with our prayer today." Refer to the *United Methodist Hymnal* for a script regarding the consecration of Communion elements.

Optional—During Communion, play Worship Clip: Y15 Choir Singing "Hallelujah," "I Believe," "This Little Light" (https://vimeo.com/132860587).

Pray together at the close of worship:

> Lord, thank you for your gift of life. I know that I can do all things through you. The power that resurrected you from the dead also lives in me. May I exercise that same power to be used for sharing your love and lighting the way. Help me see my gifts, weaknesses, strengths, community, and purpose to live according to your divine will. Allow me to stay connected to the Holy Spirit so the mountains of stuff of the world never mute your voice. I commit from this day forth to live in my call to be a disciple for the transformation of myself and the world. Amen.

Keep the commitment cards and follow up with the group participants over the next month to see how many stick with their exercises. Use them as a source of encouragement.

Go On Moment (In *FaithMinder Journals*)

"Leave the finger painting exercise behind to experience actually something that is truer, deeper, more authentic."—Sam Yun

How might God show up or act on your behalf or in your life? The promise of God is that God is always on the move, and the prevenient grace of God goes before us. God acts and works before we practice any spiritual disciplines. Yet when we practice, it provides space for us to enter into God's presence. As you continue to build spiritual muscle, always reflect on how God is working and moving in you.

Week 6: Go On Together

COACH'S PLAYBOOK

Supplies

Bible
FaithMinder Journal
Internet access and computer
Communion elements
Index cards

We are the body of Christ. We can make ourselves strong spiritually, and that personal strength translates to a stronger church. We can support one another in love. Lifting one another up builds and strengthens our spiritual muscles. We all have a purpose in the Lord, and we have a purpose in community as well. As we go on and train further, we should remember that we do not journey alone. We are a part of a community that loves us, and we can show love to others. Stay in relationship, hold one another accountable, and go on and run the race together! Love God. Love people.

We have come to the end of the six-week study, but it should not be the end of anyone's spiritual journey. We are meant to stay connected and grow together as a community of believers. This week provides a chance for reflection and worship. You already have helped create a safe place for connection, community, and love. For this session, make sure those feelings are present. Following the study, organize a small-group worship service that brings participants together as the body of Christ for Communion and prayer. If you are not able to personally bless the sacraments, invite an ordained elder to be a part of the service. Alternatively, you can have a love feast or agape meal. Read Hebrews 10 to prepare.

Foundation

So then let's also run the race that is laid out in front of us, since we have such a great cloud of witnesses surrounding us. Let's throw off any extra baggage, get rid of the sin that trips us up, and fix our eyes on Jesus, faith's pioneer and perfecter. He endured the cross, ignoring the shame, for the sake of the joy that was laid out in front of him, and sat down at the right side of God's throne.

Think about the one who endured such opposition from sinners so that you won't be discouraged and you won't give up. In your struggle against sin, you haven't resisted yet to the point of shedding blood, and you have forgotten the encouragement that addresses you as sons and daughters:

My child, don't make light of the Lord's discipline
or give up when you are corrected by him,
because the Lord disciplines whomever he loves,
and he punishes every son or daughter whom he accepts.

Bear hardship for the sake of discipline. God is treating you like sons and daughters! What child isn't disciplined by his or her father? But if you don't experience discipline, which happens to all children, then you are illegitimate and not real sons and daughters. What's more, we had human parents who disciplined us, and we respected them for it. How much more should we submit to the Father of spirits and live? Our human parents disciplined us for a little while, as it seemed best to them, but God does it for our benefit so that we can share his holiness. No discipline is fun while it lasts, but it seems painful at the time. Later, however, it yields the peaceful fruit of righteousness for those who have been trained by it.

So strengthen your drooping hands and weak knees! Make straight paths for your feet so that if any part is lame, it will be healed rather than injured more seriously. Pursue the goal of peace along with everyone—and holiness as well, because no one will see the Lord without it. Make sure that no one misses out on God's grace. Make sure that no root of bitterness grows up that might cause trouble and pollute many people. (Hebrews 12:1-15)

Reflections "Commitment"

Youth should write in the *FaithMinder Journals* for ten to fifteen minutes. Questions they can consider:

- What parts of my faith seem weak, or what are my biggest questions? What exercises would help work out those questions?
- What parts of my faith are strong and could be used to support others as they grow?
- How much time per week am I willing to give to continue my intentional discipline?

Inspire "We are Called"

Watch Inspire Clip 6 at https://umcyoungpeople.org/spiritualmuscle. Sam Yun moves us to continue the journey with the Kingdom as our goal.

Our Christian lives are called. We are called to experience change and transformation. May we stay the course and remember what matters most.

Motivate "Church on the Move"

Watch Motivation Clip 6 at https://umcyoungpeople.org/spiritualmuscle. Telley Gadson ignites us to be a church on the move. We are not just the things inside the walls; we are to go outside church walls to share the light and love all we encounter.

Spiritual Workout "Worship and Communion"

Optional—During Communion, play Worship Clip: Y15 Choir Singing "Hallelujah," "I Believe," "This Little Light" (https://vimeo.com/132860587).

Share Communion with one another in the most appropriate way for your group.

Pray together at the close of worship:

> Lord, thank you for your gift of life. I know that I can do all things through you. The power that resurrected you from the dead also lives in me. May I exercise that same power to be used for sharing your love and lighting the way. Help me see my gifts, weaknesses, strengths, community, and purpose to live according to your divine will. Allow me to stay connected to the Holy Spirit so the mountains of stuff of the world never mute your voice. I commit from this day forth to live in my call to be a disciple for the transformation of myself and the world. Amen.

Go On Moment (In *FaithMinder Journals*)

"Leave the finger painting exercise behind to experience actually something that is truer, deeper, more authentic."—Sam Yun

How might God show up or act on your behalf or in your life? The promise of God is that God is always on the move, and the prevenient grace of God goes before us. God acts and works before we practice any spiritual disciplines. Yet when we practice, it provides space for us to enter into God's presence. As you continue to build spiritual muscle, always reflect on how God is working and moving in you.

APPENDIX

PREMEETING SCALES

Supplies

Selected scales or measurement tools from the appendix, either paper or electronic copies
FaithMinder Journal

Trainer and Coach Information

By now, you have shared about the opportunity for youth to participate in *Building Spiritual Muscle.* You have gotten youth signed up and excited to grow together. These premeeting scales are designed to give you and each participant an idea of where the group is starting in terms of spiritual maturity, familiarity with faith language, and activity levels.

When trying to build muscle, add activities, and grow, knowledge is power. When initiating and sustaining change, a person has to know where he or she is starting; therefore, enter the premeeting scales and the *FaithMinder Journals.* As a trainer, you should encourage youth participants to complete at least one of the premeeting scales and set goals for their growth. You can determine which assessment is the most appropriate for your context. You can spend time talking with participants about their spiritual growth goals. They should provide you a copy of whatever assessment they take and keep a copy for themselves to refer back to once the journey has been completed.

The lower the scores or activity levels reported on these scales, the more likely it is for a participant to be a beginner in faith. The higher the scores and activity levels, the more likely a participant is already a committed follower of Christ. Beginners are exploring and need a higher level of training and attention than someone who is already following in Jesus' footsteps, or someone who is already leading others to faith.

- Choose which premeeting scales to provide to participants before the week 1 session.
- Provide participants with copies of the scales that you want them to complete.

- Ask for a completed copy back.
- After receiving a completed scale, touch base with participants to talk about their goals for growth and development.
- Keep the scales and refer back to them at the end of the materials.
- At the end of the week-six session, provide participants with blank versions of the same scales.
- Help the participants complete the assessment again, and compare their answers. This will give an indication of growth and the direction the Spirit is leading them in their faith journey.

MEASUREMENT SCALES

The following scales can be used as tools to set the baseline belief or activity level of participants at the outset of the journey.

These may also be used as follow-up scales after the end of the journey to discover areas of growth. Group leaders are encouraged to repeat usage of any premeeting scale at the end of the six sessions as a way to learn about the spiritual muscle grown by those participating in the group.

FAITH MATURITY SCALE[1]

Mark one answer for each statement. Be honest, and use your first reaction. Do not overthink the statement. Circle the number that describes how true the statement is for you.

1 = Never True 2 = Rarely True 3 = True Once in a While
4 = Sometimes True 5 = Often True 6 = Almost Always True 7 = Always True

1. I experience a deep communion with God.
   1 2 3 4 5 6 7

2. My faith shapes how I think and act each and every day.
   1 2 3 4 5 6 7

3. I help others with their religious questions and struggles.
   1 2 3 4 5 6 7

4. My faith helps me know right from wrong.
   1 2 3 4 5 6 7

5. I devote time to reading and studying the Bible.
   1 2 3 4 5 6 7

6. Every day I see evidence that God is active in the world.
   1 2 3 4 5 6 7

7. I seek out opportunities to help me grow spiritually.
   1 2 3 4 5 6 7

8. I take time for periods of prayer or meditation.
   1 2 3 4 5 6 7

9. I feel God's presence in my relationships with other people.
   1 2 3 4 5 6 7

10. My life is filled with meaning and purpose.
    1 2 3 4 5 6 7

11. I try to apply my faith to political and social issues.
    1 2 3 4 5 6 7

12. My life is committed to Jesus Christ.
    1 2 3 4 5 6 7

13. I go out of my way to show love to people I meet.
    1 2 3 4 5 6 7

14. I have a real sense that God is guiding me.
    1 2 3 4 5 6 7

15. I like to worship and pray with others.
    1 2 3 4 5 6 7

16. I think Christians must be about the business of creating international understanding and harmony.
    1 2 3 4 5 6 7

17. I am spiritually moved by the beauty of God's creation
    1 2 3 4 5 6 7

What about your faith would you like to grow or strengthen as a part of this journey?

Why are you interested in the building spiritual muscle?

[1] Benson, P. L., Donahue, M. J., & Erickson, J. A. (1993). "The faith maturity scale: Conceptualization, measurement, and empirical validation." In M. L. Lynn & D. O. Moberg (Eds.), *Research in the Social Scientific Study of Religion* (Vol. 5, pp. 1-26).

RELIGIOUS BEHAVIOR SCALE[2]

For the following 8 items, please circle how often you did each of the items during the past 12 months:

1 = Less than once a month 2 = About once a month = Two to three times a month
4 = About once a week 5 = Two to three times a week 6 = Daily

In the last 12 months, how often did you:

1. talk with another Christian about your faith, outside of a church-related context?
   1 2 3 4 5 6
2. pray alone?
   1 2 3 4 5 6
3. attend a worship service or church-related event?
   1 2 3 4 5 6
4. speak or try to speak with a non-Christian about your faith?
   1 2 3 4 5 6
5. volunteer your time to serve others?
   1 2 3 4 5 6
6. participate in a small group of your peers for religious or spiritual purposes?
   1 2 3 4 5 6
7. read your Bible by yourself?
   1 2 3 4 5 6
8. meet with a spiritual mentor (other than your parents)?
   1 2 3 4 5 6

What about your religious behavior would you like to see strengthen or grow as a part of this journey?

Why are you interested in the building spiritual muscle?

[2] Kara Powell and Chap Clark, *Sticky Faith: Everyday Ideas to Build Lasting Faith in Your Kids* (Grand Rapids: Zondervan, 2011).

PERSONAL HOLINESS ACTIVITY TRACKER

This table will help you identify how often you do exercises that strengthen your personal holiness. Personal holiness, for this scale, consists of the activities people do to show their devotion and love to God. Showing love for God is the first half of the Great Commandment (Mark 12:29-30).

How Often → Action	Every Day	About Once a Week	Every Couple of Weeks	Once a Month	Like Never
Read Scripture					
Meditate on Scripture					
Study Scripture					
Pray					
Fast					
Worship					
Live Healthy					
Share Faith					

Share Communion					
Christian Conference					
Bible Study					

Read Scripture: Reading scripture
Meditate on Scripture: Reflecting on scripture, using writing, drawing, or devices
Study Scripture: Using tools outside of scripture to better understand scripture
Pray: Spending time in personal or communal prayer
Fast: Giving up something that takes away energy for or attention to God
Worship: Experiencing God in a specifically designed space
Live Healthy: Remaining active and caring for the body
Share Faith: Talking about beliefs with others outside the church
Communion: Taking part in the Eucharist
Christian Conference: Sharing about spiritual growth with other Christians

What goals do you have for developing your personal holiness?

Why are you interested in building spiritual muscle?

SOCIAL HOLINESS ACTIVITY TRACKER

This table will help you identify how often you do exercises that strengthen your social holiness. Social holiness, for this scale, includes the activities people do to demonstrate love and care for their neighbors. Showing love for neighbor is the second half of the Great Commandment (Mark 12:31).

How Often → Action	Every Day	About Once a Week	Every Couple of Weeks	Once a Month	Like Never
Doing Good Works					
Visiting the Sick					
Visiting Prisoners					
Feeding the Hungry					
Giving to the Needy					
Seeking Justice					
Ending Oppression & Discrimination					
Addressing the Needs of the Poor					

Doing Good Works: Taking actions that demonstrate God's grace toward neighbors
Visiting the Sick: Caring for those who suffer from ailments
Visiting Prisoners: Building relationship with imprisoned populations
Feeding the Hungry: Meeting needs for the food insecure
Giving to the Needy: Giving your own time, energy, and money
Seeking Justice: Advocating on behalf of others, shining a light on systems
Ending Oppression and Discrimination: Demonstrating God's grace by standing against systems designed to create inequality or damage to others
Addressing the Needs of the Poor: Discovering the needs of the community and working to meet those needs

What goals do you have for growing your social holiness?

Why are you interested in building spiritual muscle?

CHURCH FAMILIARITY SCALE[3]

For each of the following items, answer "yes" or "no" to the questions and rank how much you agree with each statement on a scale of 1 to 5.

1 = Totally disagree   2 = Disagree Somewhat   3 = Neither Agree nor Disagree
4 = Agree Somewhat   5 = Totally Agree

Have you attended a worship service in the last 3 months?   YES   NO

I have a friend at church who is around my age.
1   2   3   4   5

I have a friend at church whom I would call an adult.
1   2   3   4   5

Have you prayed with a church staff member or minister in the last 3 months?
YES   NO

There is an adult in our church that I would call a mentor (not a pastor) for my faith.
1   2   3   4   5

My church helps me better understand my purpose in life.
1   2   3   4   5

I can name the pastoral staff at my church.   YES   NO

I have received helpful input from a pastor or church worker about my education or calling.
1   2   3   4   5

I have found a cause or issue at church that motivates me.
1   2   3   4   5

I have been on a trip or experience with my church that has helped me expand my thinking.

1 2 3 4 5

I have served the poor through my church.

1 2 3 4 5

Do you feel that you know about learning opportunities available to you at church? YES NO

Do you feel that you know about service opportunities available to you at church? YES NO

The church helps Jesus speak to me in a personal and relevant way.

1 2 3 4 5

Do you feel that you know about prayer opportunities available to you at church? YES NO

What goal would you set for yourself and the church as a part of this journey?

Why are you interested in building spiritual muscle?

[3] *"The Church Familiarity Scale" is based on Barna Research, "5 Reasons Millennials Stay Connected to Church," https://www.barna.com/research/5-reasons-millennials-stay-connected-to-church.*

COMMUNITY FAMILIARITY SCALE

For each of the following items, answer yes or no to the questions and rank how much you agree with each statement on a scale of 1 to 5.

1 = Totally disagree 2 = Disagree Somewhat 3 = Neither Agree nor Disagree
4 = Agree Somewhat 5 = Totally Agree

I know at least two of my immediate neighbors.
1 2 3 4 5

There are people in need in my community.
1 2 3 4 5

I can name the schools that are within 5 miles of my home or church.
1 2 3 4 5

I am a part of a community at school. YES NO

I am a part of a community larger than my school. YES NO

There are nonprofit organizations working in my community.
1 2 3 4 5

I know the elected officials that represent my town/county/city/district.
1 2 3 4 5

I feel comfortable communicating with elected officials about my community's needs.
1 2 3 4 5

Do you feel that you have the ability to meet some of the needs in your community? YES NO

I know how our church serves the poor and needy of my community.

1 2 3 4 5

I have seen oppression, discrimination, or injustice in my community.

1 2 3 4 5

Church helps me meet the needs of my community.

1 2 3 4 5

I know what people in my community care about.

1 2 3 4 5

What goal would your set for yourself, and the communities that you are a part of, as a part of this journey?

Why are you interested in building spiritual muscle?

USING THE COACH'S PLAYBOOK

The Coach

As participants build and strengthen spiritual muscle, they will look for encouragement, motivation, and direction. A coach can live into the support called for in Hebrews 10:24 (NIV): "Consider how we may spur one another on toward love and good deeds, not giving up meeting together, as some are in the habit of doing, but encouraging one another."

Effective coaching begins with a relationship built on trust and support. As a coach, connect with youth participants to discover their goals for spiritual growth. Great coaches are active listeners. They are supportive, patient, challenging, prayerful, compassionate, and prepared. Coaches don't do the heavy lifting for their groups. Instead, coaches understand there is a bigger picture and offer resources that help youth do their own lifting. As a leader and teacher, you as the coach can help youth discover their true purpose as disciples of Jesus Christ.

Overview

Each session includes a brief overview and learning objective for the week. Read these to keep you motivated as a coach and to give you some direction for preparation. Each session is yours to modify. Please choose to include additional scriptures and materials from other sources or add supplemental tools to meet the needs you see for your group.

Building Your Lesson

The components for your weekly study include:

- Foundation Scripture
- Reflection Journal Writing
- Inspire Video Clip
- Motivate Video Clip
- Spiritual Workout

As coach, you can rearrange or modify the components of each session to suit your group's needs. Build on the framework or focus on specific components. Lead at your own pace. Facilitate a short lesson or a long one. These components can even be incorporated or integrated with another small-group study. The possibilities are endless!

Group Dynamics

Individual spiritual growth is enhanced by a supportive community. As coach, you may want to incorporate ice breakers, team building games, or other methods for building relationships among group members. Look for opportunities to build community during the sessions. Watch for "teachable moments" where participants learn from and inspire one another. Invite the Holy Spirit in all gatherings, and follow its lead.

Prepare Your Space

Create an environment with clear expectations and trust. Participants may share private or sensitive experiences in the discussions once trust is established. Open the lesson with prayer or a song, and prepare the group to show compassion and empathy as heavy spiritual weights are lifted up by the group. Invite the group to set ground rules to foster a community of openness and sensitivity. Arrange the meeting space in a comfortable, welcoming, and inclusive manner.

Staying on Track

Spiritual Workouts encourage youth to continue their training during the week and between meetings. Before the end of each group session, review the Spiritual Workouts. Ask how youth will incorporate these challenges in their daily lives and encourage them to use their journals. Consider texting during the week to check in and motivate youth. Ask questions on social media from the previous study to keep them engaged. Use connectional tools that the youth already employ. Feel free to add activities that expand on the session to encourage personal study and reflection outside the small-group setting.

> His purpose was to equip God's people for the work of serving and building up the body of Christ until we all reach the unity of faith and knowledge of God's Son. God's goal is for us to become mature adults—to be fully grown, measured by the standard of the fullness of Christ. (Ephesians 4:12-13)

OVERVIEW FLAT PLAN

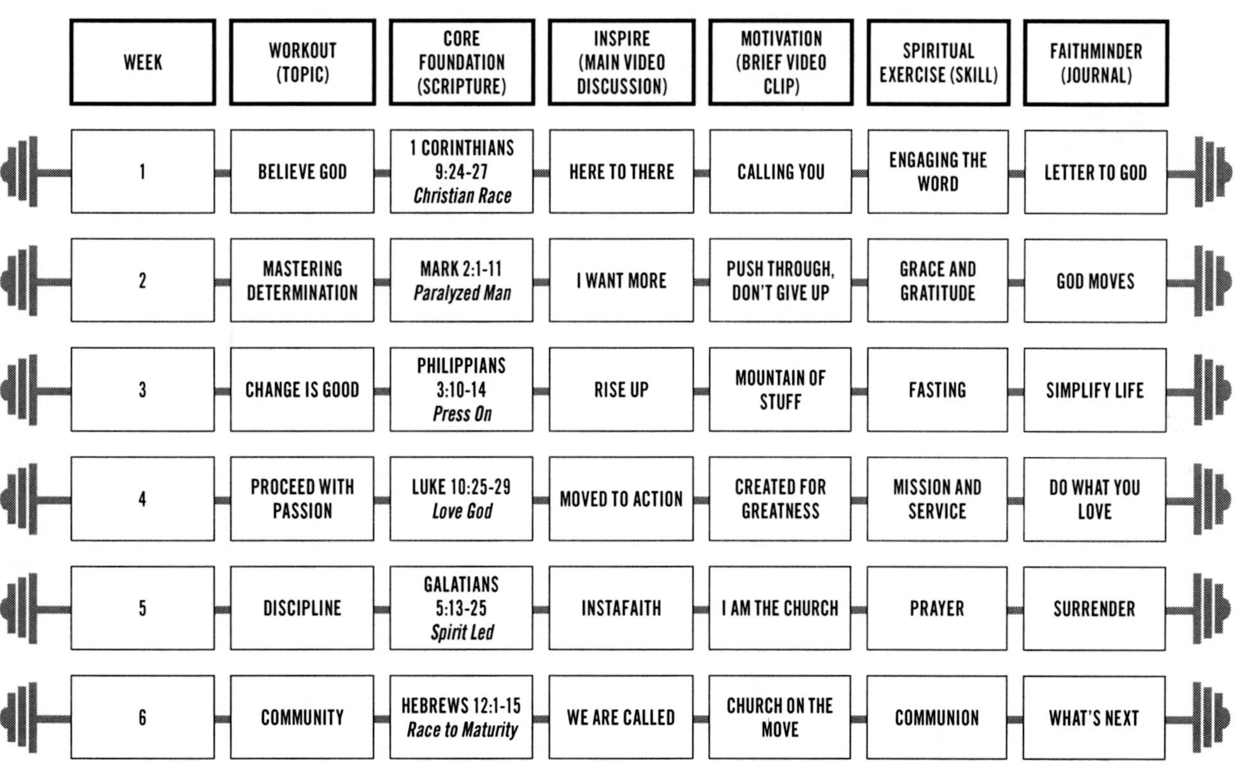

WEEK	WORKOUT (TOPIC)	CORE FOUNDATION (SCRIPTURE)	INSPIRE (MAIN VIDEO DISCUSSION)	MOTIVATION (BRIEF VIDEO CLIP)	SPIRITUAL EXERCISE (SKILL)	FAITHMINDER (JOURNAL)
1	BELIEVE GOD	1 CORINTHIANS 9:24-27 *Christian Race*	HERE TO THERE	CALLING YOU	ENGAGING THE WORD	LETTER TO GOD
2	MASTERING DETERMINATION	MARK 2:1-11 *Paralyzed Man*	I WANT MORE	PUSH THROUGH, DON'T GIVE UP	GRACE AND GRATITUDE	GOD MOVES
3	CHANGE IS GOOD	PHILIPPIANS 3:10-14 *Press On*	RISE UP	MOUNTAIN OF STUFF	FASTING	SIMPLIFY LIFE
4	PROCEED WITH PASSION	LUKE 10:25-29 *Love God*	MOVED TO ACTION	CREATED FOR GREATNESS	MISSION AND SERVICE	DO WHAT YOU LOVE
5	DISCIPLINE	GALATIANS 5:13-25 *Spirit Led*	INSTAFAITH	I AM THE CHURCH	PRAYER	SURRENDER
6	COMMUNITY	HEBREWS 12:1-15 *Race to Maturity*	WE ARE CALLED	CHURCH ON THE MOVE	COMMUNION	WHAT'S NEXT

CPSIA information can be obtained
at www.ICGtesting.com
Printed in the USA
FFOW01n0946140717
37556FF

9 780881 778625